30 Walks in New Jersey

30 Walks in

by Kevin Dann and Gordon Miller

Photographs by the authors

New Jersey

Rutgers University Press
New Brunswick, New Jersey

Library of Congress Cataloging-in-Publication Data

Dann, Kevin, 1956–
   30 Walks in New Jersey / by Kevin Dann and Gordon Miller;
photographs by the authors.
p. cm.
   Rev. ed. of: 25 walks in New Jersey. ©1982.
   ISBN 0-8135-1811-3   ISBN 0-8135-1812-1 (pbk.) :
   1. Hiking—New Jersey—Guidebooks.   2. Parks—New
Jersey—Guidebooks.   3. Forest reserves—New Jersey—
Guidebooks.   4. New Jersey—Description and travel—1981
—Guidebooks. I. Dann, Kevin T., 1956– 25 Walks in New
Jersey.   II. Miller, Gordon, 1954–   . III. Title. IV. Title: Thirty
walks in New Jersey.
GV199.42.N5D36   1992
917.49'0443—dc20   91-38199
                                     CIP

British Cataloging-in-Publication Information Available

To our parents,
Catherine and Tyler Dann
and
Galer and Inger Miller

Acknowledgments

The authors would like to express their appreciation to the many people who have assisted in the preparation of this book. Karen Reeds at Rutgers University Press was instrumental in launching this revised edition and persevered with us on the sometimes tortuous trail from *25 Walks* to *30 Walks*. Numerous rangers and other employees at the sites, as well as officials at various state and local agencies, supplied valuable information and advice. Dimitri Balomenos, Danny Burnstein, Jo Burnstein, Ian Harding, Jacquelyn Miller, Tom Slaughter, Amy Spiegel, Denise Thompson, and Kerstin Voigt contributed hours of camaraderie and many helpful suggestions on a number of the new and revised walks. Jacquelyn Miller was also responsible for bringing together the authors of this edition, and for providing companionship and encouragement along the way.

Contents

Introduction

30 Walks in New Jersey

Introduction

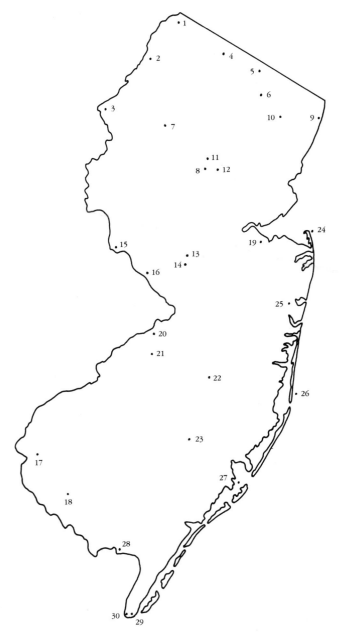

Introduction

Thirty walks in *New Jersey?* We imagine this cry of
disbelief being issued by many people, walkers and
nonwalkers alike—and perhaps for this very reason a book
such as this serves a purpose. For many people, especially
travelers who see the state from the New Jersey Turnpike,
New Jersey is the epitome of an industrial metropolis.
Many who live (or have lived) in New Jersey, however,
have an altogether different image: windswept beaches,
rolling hill country, steep talus slopes, broad green river
valleys, beaver ponds, and dense cedar swamps—these are
all part of New Jersey's landscape. There is no better way
to appreciate and understand this landscape fully than to
walk through it, and these walks are presented in that
spirit of coming to know, and hence more deeply appreciate, the land.

The walks are arranged in sections according to different
natural areas or regions. These regions are actually subdivisions of larger areas known as physiographic provinces—
areas having similar rock types, geologic structures, and
geologic histories. The physiographic provinces and the
associated natural regions in New Jersey are as follows.

The Ridge and Valley Physiographic Province

The Ridge and Valley Physiographic Province extends
from the lowland of the Saint Lawrence River south some
1,200 miles to northern Alabama. Sometimes called the
Folded Appalachians, this province is composed mainly of
folded and faulted sedimentary rocks of early Paleozoic
age. Differential erosion of resistant sandstone, quartzite,
and conglomerate and the less-resistant shale and limestone has resulted in a series of nearly parallel valleys and
ridges. In New Jersey, the Ridge and Valley Province

consists of the Kittatinny Valley, Kittatinny Mountain, and the Minisink (or Delaware) Valley. Along with the four walks in the *Delaware River Valley,* there are three walks on the *Kittatinny Ridge,* the Endless Mountain of the Lenni Lenape Indians.

New England Upland Physiographic Province

The New England Upland is the remnant of what was once a dramatic mountain system. Today, after millions of years of erosion, the roots of this mountain system survive as a series of broad ridges and narrow valleys beginning in northern New England and continuing south to Reading, Pennsylvania on the west and Manhattan Island on the east. The massive ridges of the New England Upland are composed of resistant metamorphic rocks such as gneiss and granite while the valleys are underlain by softer shale and limestone. The Reading Prong of the New England Upland extends into New Jersey as the *Highlands,* which contains the oldest rocks found in the state.

The Piedmont Physiographic Province

The Piedmont Physiographic Province stretches southwest from the Palisades along the Hudson River 1,000 miles to central Alabama. The Piedmont (literally "foot of the mountain") is gentle hill country: the farms of Bucks County, Pennsylvania, central Virginia, and a century ago, northeastern New Jersey, are all located on the Piedmont's loamy soils. In New Jersey the *Piedmont* consists of the Newark basin and its associated traprock ridges, the Palisades and the Watchung Mountains.

The Atlantic Coastal Plain Physiographic Province

The Atlantic Coastal Plain Physiographic Province, which contains about 60 percent of New Jersey's total land area, stretches from Cape Cod to Mexico. It is characterized by its level relief and its unconsolidated layers of gravel, sand, and clay. In New Jersey, the province is usually defined as having two subdivisions: the Inner and Outer Coastal Plains. Although both regions appear similar, the sediments of the Inner Coastal Plain were largely deposited during the Cretaceous period and are higher in clay content than the sandier Tertiary deposits of the Outer Coastal Plain. The walks under the *Pine Barrens,* the *Atlantic Coast* (except Gateway National Recreation Area, which is at the edge of the *Inner Coastal Plain)*, and *Cape May Region* are located on the Outer Coastal Plain.

Because the underlying geology influences topography, soil types, and even climate, it also has a direct influence on plant communities. These plant communities in turn order and define the visible landscape—be it a rocky ridge top, a barrier beach, or a salt marsh. Since these plant communities are largely defined by their most prominent components—trees—much of the description contained in each walk is devoted to characterizing and identifying the forest trees present. Each tree is identified only once, though it may occur along a dozen or more of the trails described in this book. (See the index for all instances.) Since one picture is worth a thousand words, however, it is helpful to have a pictorial guide in learning to recognize the native trees and shrubs of the state. Standard references are *A Field Guide to Trees and Shrubs* by George A. Petrides (Houghton Mifflin Co., 1972) or the *Master Tree Finder* by May Watts (Nature Study Guild, 1963). Once one learns to recognize the various trees and shrubs, one can begin to infer things about the entire community of which they are a part—which wildflowers are likely to be present, which birds might breed there, the kinds of mammals that might be found, and so on.

New Jersey's plant, animal, and mineral resources have not gone untouched, but have been exploited by man for nearly three centuries. Since a key to understanding the present landscape is to know what the past human impacts have been, many of the walks—Great Falls, Wharton State Forest, Waterloo Village, and others— illustrate the theme of resource use. In some ways, it is the underlying theme of much of the state's history, and at times it is a dismal one. It is to be hoped that these walks can help us to learn more careful stewardship of our resources by allowing us to reflect upon our past use (and misuse) of them.

Taking Care of the Land

Hiking trails (and books that describe them), by promoting the areas they traverse, sometimes run the risk of simultaneously destroying them. It is imperative that these areas be protected and preserved. Each area has its own rules and regulations; please observe these rules, as they are meant for your safety and protection as well as that of the area itself. Where there are no posted regulations, please follow these courtesies:

Don't disturb plants or animals.
Don't smoke while hiking.
Leave the trail as if nothing had been there;
    carry out all litter.

Taking Care of Yourself

If you are hiking during the warmer months of the year, especially from April to November, you are likely to be sharing the woods with another active explorer, *Ixodes dammini,* the deer tick. This tiny arachnid, often about the size of a sesame seed, can transmit the bacterial infection known as Lyme disease. Not all ticks are infected, and to pass on the disease infected ticks must remain attached for a period of several hours; a few simple precautions can help lessen the possibility of a bite. Do not brush against grass or bushes unnecessarily. Wear long pants with cuffs tucked into your socks, and keep your shirt tucked into your pants. (Light-colored clothing makes ticks easier to spot.) Check yourself regularly and use a repellant containing N–diethyl-metatoluamide (DEET). When you return home, undress and shake your clothing and then check yourself all over, looking carefully for any new "freckles." Ticks usually spend several hours searching for a place to feed, but if you find one attached, remove it with tweezers by grasping it very close to the skin and pulling it straight out. Wash the area with soap and water and save the tick in a jar for future reference. The symptoms of Lyme disease can appear from two days to a month or so after a bite. Early symptoms typically include a rash that is often ring-shaped and that slowly enlarges over several days, and flu-like conditions such as low-grade fever, chills, headache, and joint and muscle pain. Prompt treatment is important and is easily accomplished with antibiotics. A Lyme Disease Center is located at the UMDNJ-Robert Wood Johnson Medical School. The New Jersey Department of Health operates a Lyme disease hotline Monday through Friday 8:30 A.M.–4:30 P.M.: 1-800-792-8831.

Using the Book

All of the walks in this book require less than a day to complete, and many take less than half the day. The walking times indicated at the beginning of each walk are of course approximate and do not include time for lunch and rest stops. The walks are graded according to their level of difficulty (easy, moderate, difficult). The maps for each walk are schematic and often do not include auxiliary trails or certain landscape features. If you wish to obtain more detailed maps, stop at the area's visitor's center (whether an area has such a center is noted at the beginning of the walk). Topographic maps may be helpful for some of the longer walks; these are available from the following addresses (write for a state index):

Distribution Section, U.S. Geological Survey
1200 South Eads Street
Arlington, Virginia 22202

or

Bureau of Geology and Topography
Department of Environmental Protection
P.O. Box 1390
Trenton, New Jersey 08625.

If, as you walk the trails, you find the descriptions are no longer accurate, please let the authors know so that future editions can be corrected. Write them in care of the publisher.

The Kittatinny Ridge

Looking south along the Delaware River from Mount Tammany (Arrow Island in foreground), Delaware Water Gap

1. High Point State Park

Monument Trail
Distance: 3^1/$_2$ miles (Moderate)
Walking time: 2 hours
Directions: Take NJ 23 north to High Point State Park entrance. Turn right onto Kuser Rd., pass tollbooth, and follow signs to High Point Monument. Park in lot near the monument. A parking fee is charged from Memorial Day to Labor Day. (201) 875–4800.

In the extreme northwestern corner of New Jersey, along the crest of the Kittatinny Mountains, lies the state's highest elevation: High Point. Atop the 1,803-foot summit is High Point Monument, a 220-foot-tall monolith built of New Hampshire granite and locally obtained quartzite. This walk begins at this outstanding landmark, runs along a 1,700-foot-high ridge, and then leads around an extensive cedar swamp.

During the summer you may climb to the top of the monument for a spectacular view; however, the view from the base of the monument is almost as impressive. To the west lies the Minisink Valley and the Delaware River, with the ridges of the Pocono Mountains towering in the distance. Looking to the northeast one sees the Catskill Mountains, while to the southeast lies the valley of the Wallkill River. Southwest along the Kittatinny Ridge several points may be seen: the Delaware Water Gap lying forty miles away, Culver's Gap and Sunrise Mountain in the middle distance, and in the foreground, Lake Marcia and High Point Lodge. The lodge was formerly Col. Anthony Kuser's residence; it was Colonel Kuser who gave the land to the state in 1923.

Before you get on the trail, take one look to the north; on this walk you will be following the ridge that lies

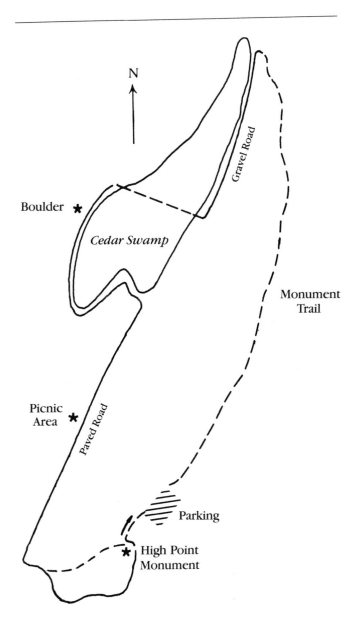

N

Boulder ★

Cedar Swamp

Gravel Road

Monument
Trail

Picnic
Area ★

Paved Road

Parking

★ High Point
Monument

directly in front of you, then descending to a valley that holds Cedar Swamp. The swamp appears as an island of conifers within the extensive deciduous woodland to the north.

As you descend the steps from the monument platform, the red-and-green-blazed Monument Trail lies to your left. When you have located the trail, follow it north (turn right). The exposed rock along the trail is Shawangunk conglomerate, which originated over 400 million years ago as fine sediments laid down in an ancient sea. The white quartz pebbles imbedded in the light-colored conglomerate rock were deposited by streams that drained into this sea. The level layers of sediments were lithified (became rock) and then folded, faulted, and finally uplifted millions of years later. The erosion-resistant conglomerate has been left as a ridge because the less-resistant sedimentary rocks adjacent to it have been worn away.

During the latest epoch of geological history, the Pleistocene, the ridge was stripped of its overlying soil by the glacial ice sheet which once covered much of northern New Jersey. This part of the ridge is still slowly regaining its soil mantle, and a few minutes spent exploring the bare rock along the trail will show how this soil-building process works.

The first plants to colonize the bare rock are crustose lichens; these appear as dark stains on the surface of the light-colored conglomerate. Lichens are actually a combination of a fungus, which provides anchorage, and an algae, which contains chlorophyll and can manufacture food for itself and its partner. This unique combination allows lichens to live in extremely harsh places such as this exposed rock. You may notice other lichens as you explore, some that are leaflike in shape and others that are branched like miniature trees. All of these lichens play an important soil-building role here on this bare rock, as they catch soil particles blown by the wind. When the lichens die, they add more material to the thin soil, allowing new plants to move onto the rock.

The next plants to arrive are the mosses, which find root in crevices in the rock where small amounts of soil have accumulated. These begin to make enough of a substrate that seeds from larger plants can take root. One of the first to do so is hairgrass, the sparse-looking grass seen scattered about the rock. Other grasses and a few species of fern join the hairgrass; most distinctive is the common polypody or rock polypody fern which spills out in evergreen mats over the rough rock. Rock polypody is readily identified by the way the leaflets are broadly attached to the main stem, and by the conspicuous round fruit dots on the underside of the leaflets.

Shrubs seen on the rock outcrops—blueberry, huckleberry, and sheep laurel in particular—eventually move in and shade out the smaller plants, creating more soil, and making way for the final stage of succession. To see this stage, continue along the trail and keep your eyes to the left. The forest here is composed of two trees that can survive the rigorous environment of this ridge top: scrub oak and pitch pine. The strong winds and icy winter conditions reduce the scrub oak to a thicket-forming shrub, and prune the windward side of the pitch pines so that they appear to be leaning uphill. The conditions for growth are so severe that seventy-year-old pitch pines may be only fifteen or twenty feet tall.

Located along this beginning section of trail are two small northern trees: striped maple and American mountain ash. The mountain ash is easily recognized from August to March by its clusters of small red fruits, and at other times of the year by its compound leaves with eleven to seventeen long, toothed leaflets. These fruits often remain on the tree all winter and are a favorite food at that time of the year for the strikingly colored evening grosbeak. Here at High Point the mountain ash is at the southern limit of its range.

High Point State Park 13

Lake Marcia and High Point Monument, High Point State Park

The striped maple, another northern species, is a slender tree with green bark marked by vertical white stripes. Its three-lobed leaves are green on both sides, though slightly paler beneath. If you look closely at both the striped maple and the mountain ash, you'll see that deer have been browsing on their twigs. Further north, the fondness of the deer's cousin the moose for striped maple has given the plant the alternative name of moosewood.

The trail passes through the parking lot and enters the woods at the rear of the lot. The woods are predominantly chestnut oak, with some red and black oaks, and occasional hickories. Though less severe than the bare rock passed earlier, this and much of the rest of the Kittatinny Ridge are dry and windswept, conditions that the chestnut oak seems better adapted to than most other trees. Under the stunted chestnut oak canopy grows an understory of sassafras, black birch, and American chestnut sprouts, and below these is a shrub layer of huckleberry, blueberry, black chokeberry, sweet fern, and mapleleaf viburnum. Occasional white birch trees grow up between the jumbled rocks on the slope to the left.

As the trail leads north, the ridge narrows to a knife-edge, allowing vistas to the east one minute, to the west the next. The trail continues $1/4$ mile and then begins to descend from the ridge. Another $1/4$ mile further it reaches a small overgrown gravel road, just before a footbridge over a stream; turn left here. A few tall hemlocks tower over a wall of rhododendron which flanks the road. At one point, there is a break in this wall, and a low-lying ridge can be seen to the right. This ridge is underlain by red sandstone of the High Falls formation (a formation is a mappable rock unit and is usually named for some distinctive location where it is found). Like the Shawangunk conglomerate, the High Falls sandstone has resisted millions of years of erosion and today makes up much of the Kittatinny Ridge.

Soon the road comes to a fork (there is a bench on the left here); bear right and follow the boardwalk into the swamp. Almost immediately after you turn you will see the cedars viewed earlier from the monument. These are Atlantic white cedars, a tree commonly found along the edges of rivers and ponds in southern New Jersey, but confined to poorly drained swamps and bogs here in North Jersey. This slender conical tree has olive green foliage with tiny scalelike needles. The spherical cones are also tiny—about $1/4$ to $1/2$ inch long. The gray, fibrous bark of the Atlantic white cedar is distinctive; it seems to twist its way up the trunk.

This cedar swamp had its origins during the close of the Ice Age, when glacial drift (rock material transported by the ice sheet) blocked a stream flowing between the two ridges and subsequently formed a pond that had no outlet. Slowly, over the last 12,000 years or more, this pond became a bog as it filled in with vegetation that formed a floating mat on top of the water. As more vegetation grew on top of the mat, plants on the underside died and fell to the bottom of the pond. Because of poor aeration, there was little decomposition of these plant remains, and layer upon layer of these remains—called peat—accumulated. With little plant matter decaying, the nutrients remained locked up in plant tissue rather than being recycled for other plants to use.

The lack of oxygen combined with the slow decay process creates an extremely acidic environment for plant growth, one that few plants can tolerate. Though the bog has matured to become a swamp with predominantly woody plants, some of the smaller plants that once covered the bog in its earlier stages are still visible. Sphagnum moss, its spongy leaves holding great amounts of water, forms hummocks throughout the swamp. On top of these sphagnum hummocks grow a number of curious insectivorous plants which can be seen along the road here. These plants obtain important nutrients they are unable to obtain from the sterile soil in which they grow— nitrogen, phosphorus, potassium, and others—from insects. The most conspicuous of these is the pitcher plant; it is identified by its tall, red-veined, purplish, tubular leaves which grow in a rosette from the base of the plant. These leaves become filled with water, making them traps for unwary insects. The inside of the leaf is very smooth, providing no foothold for the victims, and at the top of the leaf are downward-pointing hairs which help to move the insect down into the pool of water, but prevent it from moving up out of the trap. Once an insect drowns at the bottom of the pitcher, the plant secretes enzymes which digest it.

Another insect-eating plant seen here is the round-leaved sundew, although it is often overlooked because of its small size; the entire plant is only about two inches wide. Like those of the pitcher plant, its leaves have evolved to capture insects; however, the sundew's mechanism is a sticky secretion on the leaf hairs. After an insect becomes stuck, the leaf slowly folds over and digests it. It is often possible to see sundew leaves with the indigestible outer parts of the insects still adhering to them.

Just before the road emerges from the cedars and swings left, look carefully to the right; the few scrawny-looking evergreen trees here are black spruce. In northern New England and Canada, black spruce often form dense stands in bogs, but here at the southern tip of its range they occur as scattered individuals growing between the hemlocks and cedars. Some scientists believe that this and other isolated stands of black spruce are relics left from a time when the local climate was colder.

Bear left and follow along the edge of the swamp; the rhododendron and hemlock on the left contrast with the chestnut oak and low-bush blueberry on the right. The road passes a large upthrust conglomerate boulder on the right; a closer look at this boulder will reveal that the conglomerate is underlain by black shale or slate. The sediments that make up this slate were deposited during the late Ordovician period, about 450 million years ago.

The trail comes to another fork; bear left here to continue along the edge of the swamp. The rhododendron is joined by mountain laurel and swamp azalea, which combine to create a lovely floral display in June. Behind these shrubs grow cedars and occasional black spruce, while to the right grow bracken fern, scrub oak, and sheep laurel under a canopy of white and chestnut oaks. Scattered pitch pines grow on the low ridge beyond the oaks.

This corner of the swamp is more open than the area traversed so far: there are fewer trees, and the great banks of rhododendron seen earlier are absent. The trail swings left around the end of the swamp and then climbs a small knoll that gives a nice view of the swamp when the leaves are not fully out. After passing one last area of dense cedars and hemlock, the trail comes to an intersection and a stone marker indicating the Kuser Natural Area; follow the road up the hill $^1/_4$ mile, past the picnic area, and then turn left and follow the road to the monument (or pick up the red-and-green trail again on your left) in order to return to your car.

2. Stokes State Forest

Tillman Ravine
Distance: 1 1/2 miles (Easy)
Walking time: 45 minutes
Directions: Take Interstate 80 to Sparta exit. Go north on NJ 15 to US 206. Go north on US 206, 7 miles to sign for Boy Scouts camp and 4-H camp, just past the main entrance to Stokes State Forest. Turn left and go 4 1/2 miles to parking area (on left). (201) 948-3820.

A visit to Tillman Ravine is like a return to some primeval forest: 100-foot hemlocks tower overhead as you walk along a pristine brook broken here and there by waterfalls and swirling pools. The hemlock boughs scatter the sunlight into hundreds of thin rays which dimly illuminate the forest floor. There is silence, with the only exception the sound of the rushing water of Tillman Brook.

Begin your walk at the parking lot, taking the trail to the left of the trail-map sign. This trail immediately enters a stand of red and white pine, planted in 1932 by the Civilian Conservation Corps. As you walk through the pines, see if you notice a change in temperature. When you do, look up: you've left the pines behind and entered a hemlock forest. The dense foliage of the hemlock allows little sunlight to enter, and combined with the moisture from the nearby brook, it creates an area of cooler air. Such an area is known as a microclimate, a small area with a climate distinctly different from that of its surroundings. Further north, where hemlocks are more common, this cool, moist microclimate is more readily found, but here in New Jersey, hemlocks must find deeply cut, often north-facing, ravines in which to grow.

As you walk along Tillman Brook, you may be impressed by the sheer size of the trees: some hemlocks here have

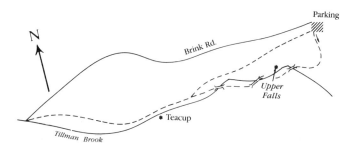

been measured to be almost 4 feet in diameter, and 112
feet in height. Most of these larger trees are well over 100
years old, and some are as old as 160 years. How have
these trees survived the cutting and burning that have
affected most of New Jersey's landscape?

Hemlocks have traditionally been protected from the ax
because the steep ravines in which they are found have
been unfriendly territory for most woodsmen. But more
than their location has kept these big hemlocks standing:
their wood is of poor quality, and the rock-hard knots can
chip the finest steel ax blade. Even today, the principal use
for hemlocks is as wood pulp. It's fortunate that such a
lovely tree has so little commercial value.

The other trees that you may see scattered through the
hemlock forest are also more typical of cooler climes:
yellow birch and American beech especially. If you look
carefully for seedlings, however, you'll notice that young
hemlocks are the most numerous. This is because once
hemlock has become established, it tends to become the
dominant tree unless disturbed. Such a forest is known as a
climax forest, because it will continue to reproduce itself
naturally. The tall mature hemlocks cast the deep shade
that is preferred by their seedlings, but that is unfavorable
to most others. In addition, the fallen hemlock needles
tend to make the soil more acid, a condition that is also
preferred by the young hemlocks.

20 *Stokes State Forest*

After you cross the first wooden footbridge over Tillman Brook, you will begin to notice numerous uprooted hemlocks lying along and sometimes across the brook and on the forest floor. Hemlocks are often toppled by wind because their roots are shallow and cannot support the weight of such large trees in a high wind. A few yards further to your right, there is an abrupt outcrop of rock that appears to be made up of horizontal bands. These bands are actually layers of sand and mud which were deposited some 400 million years ago when this area was a broad river delta only slightly above sea level. About 250 million years ago, after these sediments had been lithified to become sandstone, they were contorted when much of New Jersey experienced a period of mountain building. Occasionally, the mountain-building forces were so great that rocks at the surface were fractured. This outcrop is a good example.

A short distance further, the brook is flanked by rhododendron. The moist air and acid soil make this a suitable spot for this more southern plant. Acid-loving herbaceous plants accompany the hemlock and rhododendron here: trailing arbutus, partridgeberry, Canada mayflower, and pink lady's slippers are most common.

The dampness of the ravine is evident along here in the lush growth of moss on the soil, rocks, and fallen logs. Even the usually silver gray trunks of the beech trees have a green hue from the moss. The high humidity is especially beneficial to one group of animals in Tillman Ravine: salamanders. These small animals are often overlooked because they spend much of their time beneath rocks and fallen logs. With some careful looking, the following species may be seen in this area: the slimy salamander, red-spotted newt, red-backed salamander, northern two-lined salamander, dusky salamander, and northern red salamander.

Continue along the ravine trail to where the brook runs through a break in a sandstone outcrop. Here the rock has

Rhododendron and ferns, Tillman Ravine

again been folded to the point of fracturing, and one can see that the brook has followed the path of least resistance along this break in the rock. The stream shoots along and over the Lower Falls. Just below the falls is the Teacup, an area in the sandstone that has been scoured out by the rocks and sand carried by the brook. Such circular, smooth-sided excavations in rock are called potholes. In times when the water is low, some of the rocks that helped to form the pothole can be seen lying at the bottom.

Actually, a whole series of potholes can be seen here. Just above the Teacup is a ledge where a pothole is beginning to develop. This small pothole will gradually be enlarged by Tillman Brook. Below the Teacup is a pothole that was breached when the front of it eroded away. This former pothole appears as a semicircle.

Continue along the trail as it follows the stream down through the hemlocks. Although the ravine is a place of great quiet, you'll hear certain distinctive sounds coming from the treetops. Chickadees and nuthatches, both of which feed on the seeds of the hemlock, are usually heard as they forage about. You may hear a peculiar sound which is not as familiar: a loud chattering "chir-r-r-r, chir-r-r-r." This is the call of the red squirrel, enraged at some intruder entering its territory—probably you. If you look about, you will probably see this small, rusty colored squirrel perched on a branch, stamping its feet and jerking its bushy tail back and forth.

Like the chickadees and nuthatches, the red squirrel eats the small, winged seeds of the hemlock. To reach these seeds, the red squirrel shucks the scales off the pendant brown cones, often leaving large piles of scales on a fallen log or stump. You may come across one of these squirrel middens along the trail.

As an isolated island of northern woods, Tillman Ravine harbors a variety of interesting birds more commonly found in Vermont and New Hampshire. A large variety of warblers—small, colorful, insectivorous birds—nest here in Tillman Ravine and other hemlock woods in northwestern New Jersey, while they rarely nest elsewhere in New Jersey. Among them are the magnolia, black-throated blue, black-throated green, Canada, and blackburnian warblers and the northern water thrush. The solitary vireo, another bird more commonly found north of here, also nests in Tillman Ravine.

A little further on, the trail flattens out a little, and deciduous woods appear on the right; the white, red, and chestnut oaks remind us that we are still in New Jersey. As you continue, many signs of man's activity become apparent. The trail passes a wall of cobbled sandstone and then a stand of red cedars, both indications that this was once farmland.

As you cross over the wall to follow the brook again, notice the large sugar maple directly across the brook. If you cross the brook at this point (in times of high water this is not always possible), and follow the footpath, you will see just how close to the agricultural past you are. The open farmland spreading out in front of you here is a welcome sight after the closed canopy of the hemlock forest.

Back on the trail, more plants of deciduous woods are seen, such as blueberry, asters, Solomon's seal, and wintergreen. There continue to be signs of disturbance, however. An aspen grove and a gray birch stand suggest a recently abandoned field, as do the stone walls. When you begin to see another pine plantation like the one at the head of the trail, look carefully along the trail. The shiny, black objects you see are pieces of charcoal, and if you look closely, you can see the ruins of an old charcoal kiln to the left of the trail just before it meets the road.

The trail ends at an asphalt road, and from the bridge

here, one can watch Tillman Brook flow west to Big flat Brook, which eventually spills into the Delaware River.

The trail you've just taken is so inviting, you may want to retrace your steps on the return trip, or you can explore one of the side trails that lead away from the brook in the vicinity of Lower Falls.

3. Delaware Water Gap National Recreation Area

Mount Tammany
Distance: 3 ^{1}/2 miles (Difficult)
Walking time: 3 hours
Directions: Take Interstate 80 west past exit 4A and follow signs to the Rest Area which is the last exit before the New Jersey-Pennsylvania bridge. (908) 496–4458

Ever since the early nineteenth century, the Delaware Water Gap has attracted visitors from all over the world. Some of the earliest visitors were American landscape painters who came to paint this awesome natural wonder. Later, in 1829, the first summer resort, Kittatinny House, was built in the gap. Well-to-do vacationers would come and spend the entire summer enjoying the scenic beauty, outdoor activities, amusement parks, and dance halls of the area. By the turn of the century, transportation to the gap was better and cheaper, and many people could afford to vacation there. Dozens of resort hotels were built, and these served thousands of summer visitors.

Improved roads and air travel eventually provided people with a greater choice of vacation areas, and the resort business declined as summer-long stays were replaced by weekend excursions. The natural beauty that first attracted so many people remains, however, and in 1965 Congress authorized the Delaware Water Gap National Recreation Area to preserve the beauty of the gap and the surrounding area of the Kittatinny Ridge.

The red-and-white-dot Mount Tammany trail leaves the parking area from the back of the lot, to the left of the brown informational sign. Several trails intersect in this part of the woods, so keep your eye on the red and white blazes. The immediate steep ascent should be heeded as a

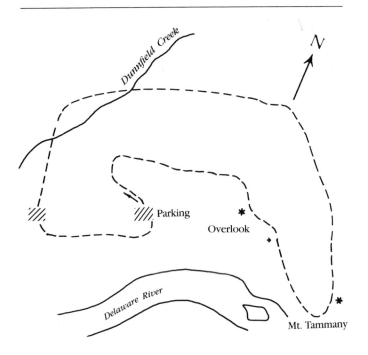

warning of what lies ahead; sturdy boots are a must for this walk. The trail climbs through woods of yellow birch and sugar maple, passing occasional large hemlocks, and then skirts an outcropping of reddish rock. This is red sandstone, the principal rock of this section of the Kittatinny Ridge. As the rivers of this region carved valleys in the softer red shale rock, ridges of erosion-resistant sandstone were left.

The trail then passes a slope covered with jumbled rock. Such an area is called a talus slope, a steep slope covered by fragments of rock from the top of the hill. Few plants or animals find this a hospitable environment, but there is one interesting animal who often makes his home here: the eastern wood rat. The wood rat looks much like the Norway rat, but can be distinguished by its longer, hairier tail, and larger ears, eyes, and whiskers. Although it is rare to see the wood rat, one can often find piles of debris and droppings near its nest, which is made in crevices among the talus.

If you are lucky, you may find a wood rat midden, which is composed of various plant materials and an assortment of strange objects. Bottle caps, nails, coins, shotgun shells, watches, keys, and other shiny metal objects are often present, along with bits of paper, rags, rubber bands, and just about anything else the animal can find. This habit of packing off such objects has earned the animal the name pack rat.

The trail becomes steeper and passes through a rocky area. Look carefully for a double red blaze noting a turn to the right where the trail crosses exposed layers of sedimentary rock; be careful not to continue straight. As soon as the trail turns, you cut across an exposed section of sandstone beds. The woods here are primarily of chestnut oak, the same ridge-top tree that grows at High Point and all along the Kittatinny Ridge.

Continue to where the trail bends left; there is an overlook here which gives a fine view of Mount Tammany, Mount Minsi (the western flank of the gap), the Delaware River, and Arrow Island below. Beyond lies the broad expanse of the Kittatinny Valley. Looking across to the base of Mount Minsi, you can see how the underlying bedrock appears to have large folds in it. These folds were caused millions of years ago, when pressures from beneath the earth contorted the bedrock into a series of great arches and troughs. In these folds lies the story of how the Delaware Water Gap was formed.

The great arches of that original landscape were huge mountains. These mountains were worn down over millions of years until this area was actually a broad flat plain lying almost at sea level. Then this plain was elevated slightly, and the rivers began to cut deeper into the land.

As they did, they caused broad valleys to form in the weaker rock, leaving the erosion-resistant rock as the Kittatinny Ridge. The Delaware River cut through the ridge at the same pace as its tributaries formed the adjoining valleys, resulting in the creation of the gap.

The trail continues along a ridge and passes over more exposed red sandstone. Here the rock has been polished by the great ice sheet that once covered the Kittatinny Ridge. To the left is a flat expanse of low-bush blueberry topped by chestnut oak, hickories, and occasional pitch pine. In fall these woods are brilliant with the scarlet of blueberry and the yellow hues of dying grasses.

After cutting across a rocky talus slope, the trail comes to a steep ledge. Though the fracturing pattern of the rock makes for good natural steps, a little rock climbing is required here. Tall hemlocks surround you as you scramble from rock to rock. It is along this part of the trail that you may catch a glimpse of another of the region's more curious mammals: the porcupine.

Occasionally, porcupines are seen waddling casually along the trail, though not commonly, since they are primarily nocturnal. If you do see a porcupine, you may be surprised at how close you can approach it; this is because porcupines are myopic. Stamp your foot, however, and the porcupine is likely to look about and bristle its quills, as he hears well and reacts quickly to touch.

At the summit of Mount Tammany, the trail bears left; continue another 1/8 mile to reach an overlook. If you are walking the trail in spring or fall, by now you have probably heard flocks of Canada geese calling as they flew by high overhead. Spend a while at this overlook, and you are sure to see a few of these flocks. Huge flocks of blackbirds can usually be seen also, and in spring a wide variety of colorful songbirds. All of this avian activity is due to the fact that the Delaware River Valley lies along the Atlantic flyway—the great invisible highway traveled twice each year by millions of birds on their way to and from South and Central America.

In autumn, you may take time here to witness the migration of the diurnal birds of prey, particularly broad-winged and red-tailed hawks. With binoculars, you can watch them as they appear as small specks in the northern sky, growing larger as they rapidly approach, then gliding by you along the ridge to the south.

For the hawks, the Kittatinny Ridge is an extremely important geographical feature. This is because westerly winds striking the flanks of the ridge produce strong updrafts that allow the hawks to soar effortlessly when conditions are right.

The view here is unobscured partly because of the type of vegetation growing: scrub oak. The scrub oak's growth is inhibited in this windy, icy spot, and so it only forms a low shrublike thicket. The trail, now marked with blue blazes, leads left off the overlook. This trail travels along the ridge for a short distance, allowing occasional glimpses of Jenny Jump and Allamuchy Mountains with the Great (Kittatinny) Valley in between. The trail soon turns left at a small open area and begins to descend the ridge along a steep, rocky trail. Before long, the woods change to sugar maple and yellow birch. Below the canopy of these trees grows a layer of smaller trees; this layer is known as the understory. In spring, the most conspicuous understory tree here is the flowering dogwood, its blossoms forming a lovely pink and white layer within the forest. In autumn, witch hazel becomes most obvious, as its scraggly yellow flowers appear in October and November.

At other times of the year, witch hazel can be recognized by its wavy-edged leaves with uneven bases, and its stubby four-part seed pods. The leaves give the plant part of its name: although it is not related to the European hazelnut, the early settlers thought its leaves resembled those of the hazel of their native land. The "witch" part of the name comes from the fact that witches rode on brooms made from the witch hazel. The early settlers used an extract from the witch hazel bark as a remedy for bruises and sprains, and made divining rods from its branches.

The trail flattens out for a short distance, giving one's legs a brief respite, then continues as a steep and rocky path for about $1/4$ mile. Here it joins the Dunnfield Creek Trail. Shortly, the trail crosses the creek via a footbridge. Dunnfield Creek drops over 1,000 feet from Mount Tammany to the Delaware River, much of it in small waterfalls like the one above the footbridge. The upper part of the creek is flanked by a steep ravine shrouded with tall hemlocks, mountain laurel, and lush growths of fern on the rock outcrops.

In another $1/4$ mile, a second trail joins from the right; this white-blazed trail is the Appalachian Trail, the famous 2,000-mile trail which goes from Mount Springer in Georgia to Mount Katahdin in Maine. Continue on the white-blazed trail, which follows high above the creek. The hemlocks are joined by American beech and yellow birch trees, with occasional large tulip trees sending their straight-as-an-arrow trunks up out of the very bottom of the ravine. Another tree that grows along here may catch your eye: the American basswood or linden tree. This tree has large heart-shaped, fine-toothed leaves. Its fragrant yellow flowers appear in early summer.

A series of pools, potholes, flumes, and waterfalls characterizes Dunnfield Creek along here as it hurries to meet the Delaware. Many of these pools are visited by trout fishermen, as this is one of the few streams in the state that supports native brook trout. The trail crosses the creek once more and leaves it behind to emerge at the Dunnfield Area parking lot. At the end of the lot, turn left to follow the road back to your car.

The Highlands

Ruins of old charcoal iron furnace. Wawayanda State Park

4. Wawayanda State Park

Cedar Swamp Trail
Distance: 5 miles (Moderate)
Walking time: 2^1/2 hours
Directions: Take NJ 23 to Union Valley Rd. near New-
foundland. Follow signs to the park. Stop at park headquarters for trail maps, if desired. Then proceed to the parking
lot at the boat launching area on Wawayanda Lake. There
is a parking fee for cars of $5.00 on weekdays and $7.00
on weekends and holidays, and for motorcycles of $2.00 at
all times. Tuesdays are free. (201) 853-4462

Here in Wawayanda State Park, close to the throngs of
civilization, are found the elements of wilderness: black
bear, beaver, bobcat, and wild turkey roam the cedar
swamps, mature forests, and rhododendron jungles of this
area. Because of its unique plant and animal life, portions
of the 10,000-acre park (including the Cedar Swamp Trail)
have recently been designated as natural areas under the
New Jersey Natural Systems Act. Parts of the trail can be
very muddy at times, so waterproof hiking boots are
advised.

"Wa-wa-yanda" is a phonetic version of a Lenape Indian
word meaning "water on the mountain." The mountain is
one of the broad gneissic ridges that make up the Highlands section of New Jersey, and the water is the beautiful
255-acre Wawayanda Lake. The lake was formerly known
as Double Pond, being two bodies of water separated by a
narrow strip of dry land. This strip can be seen today at
the center of the lake on the west side of Barker Island.
The two ponds became one in the middle of the 1800s
when the Thomas Iron Company built the dam at the
northeastern end of the lake to provide water power for its
iron operations.

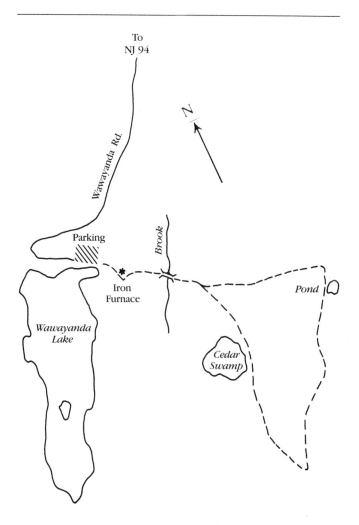

This walk begins at the dam. Leave the parking lot on the gravel road to the left and walk ¼ mile to the dam. After crossing the dam, bear left onto the dirt road and follow this path until you come upon an intersection. To the gravel road to the left and walk ¼ mile to the dam.

Wawayanda State Park **35**

After crossing the dam, bear left onto the dirt road and follow this path until you come upon an intersection. To your left are the well-preserved remains of a charcoal blast furnace where iron was produced during the late 1800s. The forty-two-foot-high furnace was built by Oliver Ames and his sons in 1845–1846. One of the sons, William, supervised the construction of the furnace, and his initials W.L.A. and the date 1846 are still visible on the iron lintel in the main arch of the furnace.

Iron ore from the nearby Wawayanda mine ($2^1/2$ miles to the northeast) was hauled by mules to this site along the road above the furnace. The massive stone wall just behind this road is the foundation of the wooden bridge that spanned the road, allowing the ore to be hauled to the opening at the top of the furnace. From here it was dumped into an iron vat at the bottom of the furnace, whose charcoal-fueled fires reached temperatures of 2,000°F. Pieces of charcoal can be seen scattered along the ground in this area.

The finished iron, in the form of rectangular "pigs," was hauled by mules to Warwick, New York, where it was shipped by railroad to the foundry. The iron from this furnace was used predominantly for casting wheels for railroad cars.

To the right of the furnace can be seen a stone-lined trench or sluiceway. Water was diverted from the creek on the right into this sluiceway to power an eight-foot-long bellows. The bellows supplied oxygen to the roaring fires of the blast furnace. Some of the firebrick which had to withstand the heat of these fires can be seen at the bottom of the main chimney.

In the woods to the right of the furnace was once the village of Double Pond, which grew up around the iron-smelting activity. At one time about 800 people lived here, and the village contained a post office, general store, creamery, blacksmith shop, cheese factory, and saloon.

After the furnace closed in 1862, the village gradually died. Today, the woods hide the remains of Double Pond's heyday. Occasionally artifacts are found that serve as reminders of the life that went on here: old cannonballs, a sled from the Thomas Iron Company, and an ice cutter from the days when Double Pond supplied the village with ice.

Continue on the trail across the wooden bridge and take the yellow-blazed Double Pond Trail to the left. Stay on this trail through the group camping area, and beyond a gate. Here you enter woods of American beech, sugar maple, and yellow birch. On the left, hemlocks squeeze their way through fractures in an impressive outcropping of gneiss.

Continue about $1/3$ mile, where the dirt road crosses over a wooden bridge. In summer, the pickerelweed and yellow pond lilies in flower make this a pretty spot. Scattered red maple snags dotted with woodpecker holes can be seen in the wet meadow on either side of the bridge. After the bridge, continue on this path, passing the red-dot trail on the right.

Soon the trail passes through a small cedar swamp, and then about 100 yards further, the blue-blazed Cedar Swamp Trail begins at the right. Take this trail, which is still more of a jeep trail than a footpath, until you come to a grove of striped maple. The trail becomes wet here, but look carefully at the muddy spots as you step over them. Deer, raccoon, and bear tracks abound. The bear tracks are unmistakable: about $3^{1}/2$ inches wide by 7 inches long. The slightly smaller tracks you may see are made by the bear's front foot, since often the round heelpad does not leave an imprint. Don't be alarmed; the largely nocturnal black bears in this area are not used to humans and will avoid encounters with them.

Listen closely here to the sound of the wind moving through the tops of the trees, which rise out of the sphagnum-moss-covered hummocks. These are Atlantic white cedar trees, somewhat out of place here, as they are usually found along the coast at much lower elevations. Man has exploited the Atlantic white cedar ever since he came to this area. The light, durable lumber was used in shipbuilding and for shingles and clapboards. During the American Revolution, white cedar charcoal was used in making gunpowder. These and other uses have had a severe impact on the white cedar forests. At present, less than 50,000 acres of cedar woods remain in New Jersey.

As you continue, look for pickerel frogs jumping between the rushes and horsetails on the trail here. Off to the side of the trail, the red fruits of the wild calla or water arum add color in the late summer, and the smell of sweet pepperbush fills the air.

The trail dries out as you leave the cedar swamp and is immediately engulfed by a dense clump of rhododendron. After the trail emerges into a clearing of ferns, it swings to the right back into rhododendron so thick that you must stoop a little as you walk. In July, the glossy leaves of the rhododendron are a backdrop for the beautiful pink and purple flowers.

Continue along until the trail drops down to a flat with an intermittent stream passing through it. Be careful not to lose the trail here; look for where the stream bed enters the woods. (The blue arrow that points to this spot is sometimes obscured in summer.) After passing through more rhododendron, the trail enters a birch-beech-maple woods that is dotted with rock outcrops. Soon the trail intersects with the yellow-blazed Banker Trail; turn left here. Look for beechdrops along this trail. This parasitic plant lacks any green pigment and is only found in association with American beech trees. Also along the ground in late summer, you'll find the shaggy husks of fallen beechnuts. These nuts provide food for ruffed grouse, raccoons, foxes, deer, squirrels, and chipmunks. Wild turkey, which were reintroduced to this area in 1970, are especially fond of beechnuts.

Where the trail comes upon another Banker Trail marker, bear left. As the trail gradually descends, different trees appear: tulip trees, sassafras, and aspen. Bear left at the fork, and continue to where the trail emerges into a clearing with a small pond. Stay to the left of the pond and follow the path into some pine woods. The trail appears to end abruptly at an asphalt road. Turn left onto the dirt road. Go $1/4$ mile, passing a few houses (the trail has left park property here), and reenter the park where the road becomes the yellow-blazed Double Pond Trail. This is the trail you began on, which will take you back to the start.

5. Skylands Botanical Gardens

Distance: 1 $^1/_4$ miles (Easy)
Walking time: 40 minutes
Directions: Take County Rd. 511 to Sloatsburg Rd.,
following signs to Ringwood State Park. Go 2 miles and
turn right at the Skylands Manor sign. The gardens are in
bloom from April to September, but the grounds are open
all year round. From Memorial Day through Labor Day a
parking fee of $3.00 on weekdays and $5.00 on weekends
is charged. Admission is free on Tuesdays. (201) 962-7031

The Skylands section of Ringwood State Park is known
more for the Skylands Manor than for the extensive
botanical gardens that surround it. The manor is an elegant
Jacobean mansion which was built in the 1920s for
Clarence Mackenzie Lewis. The finest European and
American craftsmen cut its stone and carved its elaborate
wood trim, and inside can be found sixteenth-century
stained glass windows, fireplaces, and paneling from
castles and mansions of Europe.

Plants were Lewis's hobby, and the gardens are as
fascinating as the house. Terraced gardens, a cactus
garden, a wildflower garden, and many other formal and
natural gardens are all arranged here on a 250-acre plateau
amid the Ramapo Mountains.

Begin your walk in the circular annual garden, across the
street from the manor. Mums, snapdragons, and marigolds
burst with color, joined by a variety of other flowers:
alyssum, coleus, verbena, and begonias, to name a few.
The many nectar-producing flowers attract a beautiful
array of butterflies: monarchs, spicebush swallowtails,
tiger swallowtails, and others. The annual garden is best
visited after the beginning of June, but remains colorful up
until the first autumn frost.

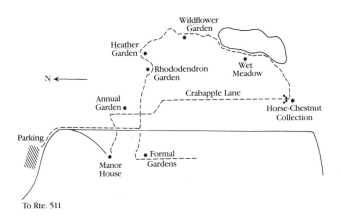

Take the right-hand pathway out of the annual garden to the perennial garden. Some of the plants here may look familiar, since many of them are typical meadow plants: goldenrod, black-eyed Susans, and wild bergamot. In August, the blue and white blossoms of the chaste tree and butterfly bush are numerous.

From the perennial garden, walk to the left and enter the "vista": a lane of crabapple trees imported from China. In early May, this lane is a photographer's delight. From the lawn here can be seen the Ramapo Mountains, where on hot August days it is not uncommon to see turkey vultures gliding over the trees, or red-tailed hawks turning lazy circles above the hills.

Continue down the lane until you reach *The Four Seasons,* a group of four statues depicting figures dressed in spring, summer, fall, and winter dress. Beyond the statues is the horse-chestnut collection. Horse chestnut trees, not native to this area, have long been used in shade-tree plantings because of their interesting leaves and fruit. Most characteristic of these trees are their seven to nine wedge-shaped toothed leaflets and their large, spiny fruits.

There are several other trees in this section of woods that

have interesting leaves and fruits. The star-shaped leaves and long-stemmed, prickly fruits that look like a medieval knight's mace belong to the sweet gum tree. The tree gets its name from the sap that exudes from the wounds, and this hardened sap, or gum, is chewed by some people. The straight, tall tree with the peculiar four-pointed leaves is the tulip tree, also known as the yellow or tulip poplar. This tree gets its name from the large tuliplike orange and green flowers which can be seen in May and June. Its fruits are born in upright conelike structures which often remain on the tree throughout the winter. These seeds are eaten by squirrels and a number of birds. The wood of the tulip tree is soft and straight-grained and thus easily worked. In the past, Indians turned the trunks of tulip trees into dugout canoes, while today the wood is used for making furniture, tools, and toys.

The large nuts that you may see along the ground here come from the pignut hickory tree. This tree has compound leaves bearing five leaflets which turn bright yellow in October. The large nuts are eaten by squirrels, chipmunks, and deer mice, and it is possible to tell who has been eating the nuts by the way they've been opened. If you find a nut cut into many pieces, this is the work of a gray squirrel or chipmunk. If the nut has one smooth elliptic opening, however, you have found the work of the flying squirrel, which is rarely seen because of its nocturnal habits. Deer mice open the nuts from two sides.

These three trees—the sweet gum, tulip tree, and pignut hickory—are trees of the southern forest; that is, they are toward the northern end of their range here. In this same small section of woods are also trees more representative of the northern woods. Sugar maple can be recognized by its dark brown bark marked with vertical grooves and ridges and five-lobed leaves. This tree is as valuable for its lumber as it is for its sap, which is collected to make maple

Old pumphouse, Skylands Manor

syrup. Another northern tree seen here is the larch or tamarack, which is the only northern conifer that sheds its needles in autumn. Two other conifers, red and white pine, also grow here. The two are easily distinguished by both their bark and their needles. The bark of the red pine is reddish and scaly, while that of the white pine is dark with deep furrows. White pine has needles in clusters of five, red pine, of two.

Go to the left, passing by a group of red pines, and follow a grassy lane to Swan Pond. The small, man-made pond is dotted with fragrant water lilies and bullhead lilies in summer. Forget-me-nots grow along the edge of the pond among the grass and reeds. A closer look here will reveal the discarded exoskeletons of dragonflies and damselflies, which can be seen darting above the water.

These are left behind after the aquatic nymphs leave the water and emerge via partially submerged plants as winged adults.

On the other side of the pond are a small clump of rhododendron and one of weeping birch trees. These trees are often used as perches by kingbirds, which sally out over the water to snatch up insects. Growing along the near side of the pond are alders and willows, both typical of wet areas like this. The tall plant with whorled leaves and the domed cluster of pinkish flowers that grows along the path here is spotted joe-pye weed. The wet meadow harbors several other plants that prefer moist soil: sensitive fern, marsh fern, and various orchids. At the end of the pond, the trail becomes quite mucky. Watch your step!

Proceed to where the trail splits and take the right-hand fork, which loops around toward a small creek. Take a left before the stone bridge and enter the wildflower garden. In June, the fragrance of sweet bay magnolia fills the air here, giving way to the aroma of sweet pepperbush in July and August. An incredible variety of native wildflowers and ferns has been assembled in this garden, and the identification labels on each of the plants make this an excellent place to become familiar with native plants.

Many of the plants growing together here would not be found growing together in the wild. While Indian pipe and rattlesnake plantain orchids are found in woods all through the northeast, bunchberry, another plant growing here in the wildflower garden, only grows in the far north or in the mountains further south. Some of the plants growing together here have widely different soil acidity requirements. Many among them—wintergreen, pink lady's slipper, Canada mayflower, partridgeberry, and Indian cucumber root, for example—prefer quite acidic soil. A few others grow only in sweet soil, soil that is neutral or basic. Dutchman's-breeches, columbine, and some of the ferns—maidenhair, spleenworts, and purple cliffbrake—prefer such conditions.

At the end of the wildflower garden is a wet area of ferns and cattails. Bear right, then left along the pond. This pond, which abounds with frogs and muskrat, is surrounded by sweet pepperbush, Saint-John's-wort, buttonbush, and rose of Sharon, all of which bloom in late summer. In early spring, even before the leaves are out, the drooping white flowers of the shadbush are seen here. This shrub gets its name from the fact that its flowers appear when the shad move up coastal streams to spawn.

Beyond the pond is the "moraine garden," which contains plants that thrive under the hot, dry surface conditions typical of talus slopes and rocky areas in alpine regions. These plants have roots that grow deep to tap water well below the surface. Here in the garden, this condition is recreated by burying concrete water tanks which can be replenished. Most of the plants growing here are heathers: their tiny leaves and prostrate growth habit are typical of alpine plants. The heathers grown here are from all over Europe: England, France, Belgium, and the Netherlands.

The next stop, the rhododendron garden, should be visited in June when the many-colored rhododendron blossoms are joined by azalea and mountain laurel flowers. From here, walk through the perennial garden and across the road to the magnolia walk, which is especially beautiful in June. Next, pass through the summer garden, which is filled with a variety of flowers. As you walk through, see if you can guess how each flower gets its name—bee balm, wormwood, beardtongue, alum root, bellflower, tickseed, and mistflower.

As you finish your walk at the peony garden and return to your car, try to picture the gardens in the era when Clarence Mackenzie Lewis had scores of gardeners maintaining the grounds. Today, the state must make do with a very small staff, assisted by volunteers from the Skylands Association.

6. Ramapo Mountain State Forest

Ramapo Lake
Distance: 4^1/$_2$ miles (Difficult)
Walking time: 3 hours
Directions: Take US 202 to Oakland. At the railroad tracks, turn onto W. Oakland Ave., and when you come to a T, turn right onto Skyline Drive. Go 1^1/$_4$ miles to the parking lot on the left at the top of the hill, across the road from Camp Tamarack Boy Scout Camp. (201) 337–0960

Just before you begin to ascend Skyline Drive, you cross the scenic Ramapo River; in one sense, this walk begins there. The Ramapo (a Lenape Indian name meaning "formed of round ponds") flows along the Great Border Fault, where 200 million years ago the earth's crust to the west of the fault was uplifted. The mountains that were formed have been greatly eroded since then, producing the Highlands, a range of ridges and plateaus of which the Ramapo Mountains are a part.

The rocks of the Highlands are truly ancient. Some 1.2 *billion* years ago, these rocks had their beginnings as sediments being deposited in a vast undersea basin. Mudstone and shale were gradually formed from these sediments, then later subjected to ages of intense heat and pressure, producing the extremely hard rock called gneiss. This ancient rock can be seen exposed at many places along this walk.

From the parking lot, walk past the gate and follow the asphalt road to the yellow-blazed trail leading off to the left. The trail begins as a wide, level path, but be advised that it becomes much more difficult later on; sturdy shoes are strongly recommended.

Almost immediately after you enter the trail, there is a large outcrop of gneiss on the right. If you are carrying a

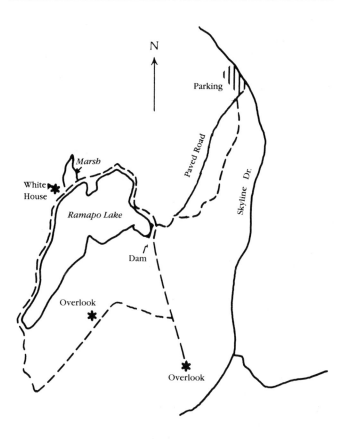

compass, hold it up to a section of this rock and see what happens. If the needle spins out of its normal position, you've found a deposit of iron ore, or magnetite. These deposits are found throughout the Ramapo Mountains and are believed to have been introduced into the surrounding metamorphic rock during volcanic activity deep below the surface. In addition, iron oxide deposits are found locally; these are produced by weathering of the magnetite. These deposits were mined from the beginning of the 1700s until quite recently, although maximum production was reached around 1880.

This and later sections of the trail are part of the old Cannonball Road, along which lie many old iron mines; some of the roads that served these mines became part of a road used by the Continental Army during the Revolutionary War to transport munitions—hence the name Cannonball Road. This mountainous route afforded safety from British attacks on vital supplies of weapons and ammunition.

Continue along the trail, bearing right at a fork that leads downhill. Just before the trail joins a paved road, bear left. There are numerous downed trees here, which give evidence that you are walking along a ridge top: the trees here are exposed to the winds and are toppled more frequently than those growing on the protected slopes below.

Many of these windblown trees have been worked by pileated woodpeckers, whose large, characteristically rectangular excavations in search of carpenter ants can be seen in some of the dead trees lying along the trail. Although the pileated woodpecker is not often seen, its relative the common flicker is frequently seen searching the ground for ants and beetle larvae. Its loud "wicker" call, golden wing linings, and white rump patch make the flicker unmistakable.

The trail passes a number of large tulip trees, and then along a small ravine flanked by ferns. Shortly it crosses a creek and through an area of jumbled fractured rock.

The minerals that make up the gneiss in these rock outcrops are arranged in parallel layers, and as the rock weathers, it tends to break up along these layers into angular blocks. A strikingly different type of rock, which is speckled with white pebbles, can be seen occasionally along the trail here. This is Green Pond formation conglomerate, made up of hard reddish-purple sedimentary rock containing pebbles of white quartz. If you were to

48 *Ramapo Mountain State Forest*

Waterlily, Ramapo Mountain State Forest

look for the source of this rock, you would have to look
some ten miles to the northwest, to Schunemunk Mountain. The pieces of conglomerate rock in the Ramapo
Mountains were plucked from Schunemunk Mountain
more than 10,000 years ago, then carried by the ice to
their resting place here. Such glacially transported rocks
are known as erratics, since they are dramatically different
from the underlying rock.

The trail passes into an area with a number of chestnut
oaks. The chestnut oak is most easily identified by its
leaves, which have seven to seventeen pairs of rounded
teeth, and its dark, deeply ridged bark. The chestnut oak
survives better than most trees on the thin, dry soils of the
northern New Jersey ridgetops, and is thus characteristic
of the upland forest along these mountains.

Underneath the chestnut oaks here, and in most places
where it is the dominant tree, very few shrubs or wildflowers grow. The acid-loving heath shrubs such as blueberry,
huckleberry, and mountain laurel are found, while bracken

Gneiss outcrop, Ramapo Mountain State Forest

fern, goldenrod, and asters are the most commonly seen herbaceous plants.

The trail continues through a thicket of mountain laurel, past an interesting rock outcrop, and then emerges onto a paved road. Bear left here and go down the hill until you reach the dam. This dam was built by a group of sportsmen who bought the area to create a lake for fishing. At that time, the area was known as Rotten Pond. This name came indirectly from the Dutch settlers who first lived here, who called it "rote" (rat) pond. The "rats" were muskrat which they trapped here. Today, Rotten Pond is Ramapo Lake, a peaceful mountain fishing spot.

Before the dam, bear right and follow the road that goes around the lake. The ruins of a large stone building known as The Castle can be seen on a nearby hill. Built in 1910, the building was destroyed by fire in 1962.

Continue to a fork in the road and bear left. The road soon passes a white house and then forks again; bear left again. A short detour to the left along any part of this section of the road gives an excellent view of the southern end of the lake. This end is very shallow, and during dry periods, old tree stumps can be seen sticking above the water. Great blue herons, green herons, wood ducks, and mallards can usually be seen feeding among the purple-flowered loosestrife and pond lilies along the edge of the lake here.

Return to the road and pass a grassy path that leads to the right. About 100 yards further, the road forks again. Bear right onto a broken-up asphalt road. Just as this road makes a horseshoe bend downhill, take the yellow-blazed trail through the woods to the left. Follow this trail as it descends sharply toward a creek. Cross the creek and then scramble alongside of an outcrop. There are both yellow and red trail markers on this section of the trail.

The trail emerges onto the first of a series of overlooks. The town of Oakland is to the left. Crystal Lake is below, and in the distance to the right, the northernmost portion of the first Watchung Mountain.

Follow the yellow-blazed trail which skirts a ledge, and as the trail goes up over more rock, look back to see the long, narrow form of Lake Inez. A short distance further, the trail comes to a small stand of pitch pine and scrub oak. These two trees replace the chestnut oak on a very few ridge tops in the state, where they must withstand not only thin, dry soil, but severe climatic conditions. Strong winds, frequent sleet and ice storms, and periodic fires make this a tough spot for any tree to grow. Note how the pitch pine clings to the rock.

A few chickadees may be seen on these ridge tops but little else in the way of bird life. Dense foliage and water are a requirement for most birds, and neither of these requirements is met on these dry, sparse ridge tops.

The trail leads to another outcrop, with good views to the west toward the Wyanokie Plateau. From here, cross over the back of the rock and reenter the woods. The trail forks—take the red trail to the right—and then comes to

Ramapo Lake, Ramapo Mountain State Forest

another fork in $^1/_2$ mile. Bear right and follow the trail a short distance to the final overlook. Pale corydalis, a relative of wild bleeding heart, grows on this outcrop.

Retrace your steps to the fork and bear right. You may notice that the trees are slightly different along the trail here, and that it is generally cooler and wetter than on the previous section of the trail. This is a north-facing slope, and as such is protected from the sun's dessicating rays. The relatively moist conditions that prevail here support a greater variety of trees, shrubs, and wildflowers.

The trail continues down the hill to an even moister area; the reed grass, ferns, witch hazel, and even skunk cabbage seem a welcome relief after the dry sparseness of the ridge tops.

A short way further, the trail comes out at the dam. From here, follow the road back to the parking lot.

7. Waterloo Village

Distance: 1^1/$_2$ miles (Easy)
Walking time: 3 hours
Directions: Take Interstate 80 to exit 25 in Stanhope. Go
north 1 mile on US 206, turn left on Waterloo Rd., and
continue about 2^1/$_2$ miles. The village is open from mid-
April through December, Tuesday to Sunday from 10:00
A.M., to 6:00 P.M. (until 5:00 P.M. from October through
December). It is closed on Easter, Thanksgiving, and
Christmas, and is open on holiday Mondays and closed the
following Tuesdays. The fee for adults is $6.00 on week-
days and $7.50 on weekends, for senior citizens $4.50 on
weekdays and $5.00 on weekends, and for children 6-12
years $3.00 at all times. A large portion of the village is
accessible to wheelchairs and strollers. (201) 347-0900

Once described as "the only first-class ghost town in the
northeastern United States," Waterloo Village is coming to
life again as a living museum of New Jersey's past. This
walk through the restored village and along the towpath of
the Morris Canal takes you through more than a century of
fascinating American history. The walk gives one a sense
of the forces that change people's relations with the land,
and with each other.

Although some of the buildings within the village are
closed to the public, the majority are open, and are staffed
with interpreters who can describe in detail the activities
associated with their particular building. It is suggested,
however, that one begin or end with this walking tour to
help fit together the pieces of this historical jigsaw puzzle.

From the parking area, walk past the concert area to the
herb garden. Herbs from the garden were put to many
domestic uses; to find out more about these uses, stop at
the next building. Formerly a "gentleman's barn" from

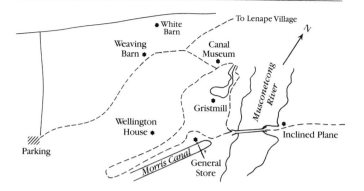

Victorian times, this barn now houses an apothecary shop and herb-drying rooms. Next, you pass a barn that houses an Indian Museum and Gift Shop and, on the lower level, a carriage collection. You then pass another barn, which now houses textile artisans.

You can continue past the white barn and turn left to go to the recently constructed Lenape Indian Village on an island in Waterloo Lake. Here many of the Lenapes' activities, artifacts, and architecture are re-created, thus providing a glimpse into what the daily life and culture of these early inhabitants were like some 400 years ago.

Alternatively, at the white barn, you can turn right and follow the road, which leads toward the river, and then bear right. The road passes a row of imposing buildings: the Iron Master's house, the Peter Smith house, the Miller's house, and the Stagecoach Inn and Tavern. Continue past the Homestead, a stone horse barn which was converted to a home in the early nineteenth century. After the Homestead, the road passes the Wellington house, the Canal house, the Nathan Smith house, and finally the Methodist Church.

At the Methodist Church, turn and retrace your steps, this time following the waterway to your right. This is a section of the Morris Canal, which was the principal reason for the growth and development of the town of

Waterloo. The canal, which went from the Delaware River at Phillipsburg to the mouth of the Hudson at Newark, was completed in 1831.

The Morris Canal was largely built to supply fuel to the many iron forges and furnaces located throughout the New Jersey Highlands. The fuel, anthracite coal, could be easily obtained from the Lehigh Valley just across the river from Phillipsburg. The coal was transported in long, narrow barges called canal boats, which were pulled along by mules. These boats carried up to seventy-five tons of cargo, which included grain, wood, bricks, and lumber as well as coal and iron ore. With such heavy loads, the boats traveled at less than two miles per hour, and the complete journey took five days.

The stone building you come to was a general store, built here on the bank of the Morris Canal in 1831. The canal boats could float right up to the store's back door, and the drivers could conduct their business without ever setting foot on land. Many boats went by each day, and the store was a successful business venture for the Smith family, who built many of the homes that you have passed on your walk through the village.

Just past the general store is guard lock 3 west of the Morris Canal. This guard lock is actually a combination masonry lock and wooden aqueduct which carried boats over the mill tailrace (to the left) and into the lock pond (at the right). The building to the left of the lock is a blacksmith's shop which records show to have been operating as early as 1790. After 1831, the shop's business boomed, because the canal mules were constantly in need of new shoes.

Follow the wooden bridge across the lock pond to the other side. The cleared path that lies ahead is inclined plane 4 west of the Morris Canal, which was recently named a National Historic Engineering Site by the American Society of Civil Engineers. This and the twenty-two other inclined planes along the length of the Morris Canal

General store at Waterloo Village (Morris Canal in foreground)

were built to haul the canal boats up hills that could not
be easily circumvented. Via the thirty-four locks and
twenty-three inclined planes, a boat traveling between
Newark and Phillipsburg was lifted and lowered some
1,674 feet.

How was the seventy-five-ton canal boat moved up this
hill, which has a vertical rise of eighty feet? Walk up the
plane, and you will notice smooth granite blocks imbedded in the path. These huge stone "sleepers" were the
foundation for a boat railway; the holes in the face of the
granite blocks are from the rivets that once held the tracks
in place. A large wooden plane car or cradle slowly made
its way up the inclined plane. The canal boat entered the
cradle in the lock pond below, as the canal mules were
unhitched after crossing over the wooden bridge.

The power for this boat railway came from the canal
above the inclined plane. A flume carried water from the
canal to a penstock, a long vertical conduit which led to a
turbine. The weight of the falling water turned the turbine,

which through a series of gears wound a cable around a steel drum twelve feet in diameter. The cable, attached to the plane car, drew the heavy load to the top of the plane. After the plane car reached the top, the boat reentered the canal.

Where the inclined plane path ends, look for a footpath leading to the right of the canal. This is the old towpath, which can be followed for a few hundred yards through the woods.

When the canal was operating, this land was all open farmland. Because so much land had been cleared of timber, firewood was in short supply, and farmers along the canal took advantage of the plentiful supply of coal which floated by each day on the canal boats. Many would barter produce for the coal, but some had craftier methods. A common trick was for a farmer to set up bottles as targets for the canal boatmen, who would throw pieces of coal at them.

After $1/4$ mile or so, retrace your steps to the inclined plane. The high stone embankments on either side of the wide path are a visible reminder of the force that led to the decline and eventual abandonment of the Morris Canal. A trestle of the Sussex Railroad, which was built in 1854, used to span these embankments. The railroad could carry iron and coal more quickly and cheaply than the canal boats could, and by 1900, the Morris Canal had become obsolete.

Cross over the bridge again and turn right along the water. To the right is the Musconetcong River, and to the left, the millpond of the gristmill and sawmill. At the far end of the millpond, you pass a grassy mound; this is all that remains of the Andover Forge, which was built in 1760. The forge processed pig iron from Andover Furnace seven miles to the north. By heating the iron and then pounding it with a great iron hammer, which was activated by a waterwheel, the iron was made stronger. The forge's four hammers weighed five hundred pounds each, and the waterwheel that drove them was twenty-five feet in diameter. As was true of many of the forges and furnaces in northern New Jersey, the Andover Forge became an important source of iron and steel for armaments used by the Continental Army during the Revolutionary War.

Continue to the end of the peninsula and cross over to "shore" again. Ahead of you lies a small building which houses the museum of the Canal Society of New Jersey. A visit to the museum makes a good final stop on your walk through Waterloo Village. Here you can see photographs and a videotape of the canal boats and boatmen, a variety of artifacts associated with canal life, and even a scale model of the inclined plane seen earlier on the walk.

8. Scherman and Hoffman Wildlife Sanctuaries

Distance: $2^1/_2$ miles (Moderate)

Walking time: $1^1/_2$ hours

Directions: From the north, take Interstate 287 to exit 26B (marked Bernardsville and US 202); from the south, take 287 to the second Maple Ave. exit (marked N. Maple Ave. and US 202). Proceed to the traffic light at US 202 near an old stone mill. Go straight at this light onto Childs Rd. Continue about 100 yards to a fork and bear right onto Hardscrabble Rd. Go to the visitors' parking lot, which is 1 mile ahead on the right, just past the main entrance to the sanctuary. The sanctuary trails are open from 9:00 A.M. to 5:00 P.M. every day except holidays. The nature center is open Tuesday through Saturday from 9:00 A.M. to 5:00 P.M. and Sunday from noon until 5:00 P.M. (908) 766-5787

The Scherman and Hoffman wildlife sanctuaries, operated by the New Jersey Audubon Society, comprise about 250 acres in the southeastern corner of the Highlands. The short, relatively easy trail loop and small nature museum make for a pleasant morning's visit, especially for families.

From the back of the parking lot, follow the red-blazed Dogwood Trail up the rocky slope. On this lower part of the slope grow red, black, and white oaks, red maples, sugar maples, and tall tulip trees. The fast-growing tulip trees, though not most numerous of the species present, seem to dominate the forest on this slope, since they tower over the oaks and maples. However, their seedlings cannot thrive in the shade cast by the growing forest, which if left undisturbed, may come to be dominated by sugar maple, whose seedlings are shade tolerant. Though the mature tulip trees may retain their positions by virtue

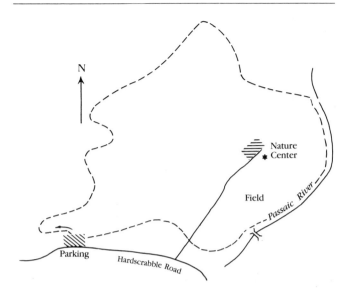

of a few feet advantage in height, this great height often dooms them, for the brittle wood is susceptible to damage by wind and lightning.

The trail makes a number of switchbacks as it continues up the slope. The angular blocks of gneiss scattered about indicate that you are still in the Highlands, though this area differs from the other walks in the Highlands in that it is south of the area that was covered by the most recent glacial advance, the Wisconsin ice sheet. This makes for subtle differences in the terrain along this walk; there are not the ice-polished outcrops seen in the Ramapo Mountains to the north, and the soil along the ridge here is deeper, not having been scraped away by the glacier.

This trail gets its name from one of the understory trees growing below the forest canopy, the flowering dogwood. This small tree, which rarely exceeds thirty feet in height and eight inches in girth, is one of the first understory trees to appear in the growing forests throughout much of the state. It usually persists as a component of the understory even after the forest has reached the climax stage.

Flowering dogwood is identified by its dark, deeply checkered bark and by its broad, elliptic leaves with five to six pairs of veins. In autumn these leaves turn deep scarlet, thus outlining the understory layer quite distinctly. (Fall is a good time of year to become acquainted with the common trees and shrubs, as their colors allow you to study their distribution from a distance.) Equally distinctive are the flowering dogwood's deceptive "flowers": its showy white petals are actually modified leaves or bracts, and the flowers (more properly called "florets") themselves are clustered at the center. The flowers develop into bunches of red berries in the fall, and these form an important source of food for a variety of animals during the colder months: ruffed grouse, cardinals, evening grosbeaks, and gray squirrels in particular. The dogwood was an important tree to our colonial forefathers also, not for its berries, but for its hard, dense wood. Dogwood was used by them for making tool handles, sled runners, and shuttles for weaving, since its close-grained wood has the quality of becoming smooth with use.

The trail continues up the slope, passing a few American beech trees along the way. The American beech is unmistakable because of its smooth, gray bark. One of these beeches along the right side of the trail has grown up around a large gneiss boulder. There is a space between the tree and the rock where squirrels often cache seeds from nearby beech and tulip trees. Toward the top of the ridge, the trail passes a clump of blackberry bushes. From a crack in a gneiss outcrop near these bushes grows ebony spleenwort, a delicate fern with shining dark stems. While many of the spleenworts prefer shaded areas with sweet (basic) soil, the ebony spleenwort thrives in slightly acidic soil and can even tolerate full sun if there is enough moisture.

Flowering Dogwood, Scherman Sanctuary

The trail passes an old stone wall, a reminder that this ridge was once cleared of its vegetation. Near the wall are a number of bleached and broken American chestnut stumps. The chestnut was once a very common tree with a range that included most of the eastern third of the United States. It was an extremely valuable tree also: the decay-resistant wood was in great demand for furniture, musical instruments, and railroad ties, and the nuts were both an important wildlife forage and a delicacy for people. In 1890, a fungal blight was accidentally introduced into the country on infected nursery trees brought into New York City from China. From New York the blight spread at a rate of about twenty miles per year, so that by 1920 it had destroyed virtually every chestnut tree in the northeast.

Though no longer a significant component of the northeastern forest, the chestnut has not disappeared completely. Today it survives as an understory tree, sprouting from the roots and stumps of older blight-killed trees. Just as these sprouts reach the point of flowering and fruiting, however, the blight, visible as a ring of orange blisters on the lower trunk, takes hold and quickly kills the tree.

Here toward the top of the ridge, chestnut oak and black birch become more common than on the slopes below. Chestnut oak is the familiar ridge-top tree common throughout the Highlands and along the Kittatinny Ridge. The black birch is easily recognized by the smooth, shiny, almost black bark on younger trees; on older trees the bark becomes scaly and breaks up into plates much like its relative the river birch. The light-colored horizontal markings, called lenticels, serve as pores, allowing gases to pass through the outer bark of the tree. These lenticels become stretched as the tree grows, causing the bark to peel off in some places. (This is more noticeable on white and yellow birch.) Black birch is often called sweet birch, because its twigs contain oil of wintergreen; a mild tea can be made by steeping the young twigs in boiling water.

64 *Scherman and Hoffman Sanctuaries*

As you cross the top of the ridge and begin to descend, to the right of the trail there is a distinctive black birch tree which has "merged" with a tulip tree, probably after having been knocked over in a storm. The tulip tree has grown a burl of woody tissue to protect itself from the abrasion caused by the birch trunk, and has sent one of its branches skyward to catch more light than its downward-tilted branches can receive.

The struggle for sunlight is evidenced by another plant along the trail here, the wild grape. This familiar vine is commonly found on abandoned agricultural land, since often birds and mammals will drop grape seeds in old fields. This is how these vines began; after being transported to this field and dropped, they germinated and grew until they climbed onto nearby young trees and shrubs. In their vigorous fight to remain in the sunlight, these vines have reached upward with the trees as they grew. The special mechanism that allows the grapevine to do this is its tendrils, slender twining outgrowths of the stem. Another vine growing nearby, which contrasts with the grape in its method of climbing, is poison ivy. It makes its way skyward by means of small aerial rootlets which become attached to the bark of the tree. These rootlets can be readily seen as the dense covering of dark fibers along the poison ivy stem.

The trail passes over another stone wall and continues downhill past some large snags bearing rectangular excavations, suggesting that they have been worked over for carpenter ants by a pileated woodpecker. This side of the hill, facing north, is noticeably cooler than the south side, where the trail began. This partially accounts for the difference in vegetation along this part of the trail: iron-wood, a moisture-loving tree that is part of the understory here on the lower portion of the north slope, was not present on the warmer, drier south slope.

Where the trail forks, swing left and follow the trail along the Passaic River. The Passaic is more like a brook here, perhaps less than a mile from its headwaters. From here it travels through the Great Swamp and then flows north until it reaches other branches within the Watchung basin. The Passaic eventually drains through the Second Watchung Mountain at Little Falls, and makes its final escape through the first Watchung Mountain at Great Falls in Paterson.

The trail follows the river through cool woods of beech and yellow birch, the ground carpeted in some places with lush growths of fern. The trail leads to the right across a slightly dilapidated footbridge before emerging into an open field. Turn left at the T and follow this field trail around to the entrance road. The Nature Center, housing wildlife displays and a bookstore, is at the end of this road to the right. To return to your car, continue on the Dogwood Trail across the entrance road and back to the parking lot.

The Piedmont

Pickerelweed, Lord Stirling Park

9. Palisades Interstate Park

Distance: 5 miles (Difficult)
Walking time: 2¹/₂ hours
Directions: Take the Palisades Parkway to exit 2 and follow
the signs to the park entrance. Follow road past park
headquarters to Alpine picnic area. A parking fee of $2.50
is charged from April 1 to October 31. (201) 768-1360

As you enter the parking lot, notice the reddish sandstone
walls along the rear of the lot. Some 190 million years ago,
while this sandstone was being formed, molten rock was
forced upward through its horizontal layers to form a long,
narrow, vertical sill. The softer sandstone has been eroded
away, leaving the forty-mile long monolith known as the
Palisades, named for its resemblance to a palisaded village.
The Indian name for this ridge, Weh-awk-en, describes its
appearance equally well; the middle syllable "awk" means
"rocks that resemble trees."

Begin your walk at the end of the parking lot, where a
gravel path leads past a white house on the left. The
house, known as Cornwallis Headquarters, was a riverside
tavern that served riverboat captains and their crews. On
November 19,1776, Lord Cornwallis and some 5,000
British and Hessian soldiers crossed the Hudson from the
New York side and scaled the cliffs at Closter Landing in
order to surprise Gen. George Washington and his men
who were encamped at Fort Lee and Hackensack. It is
thought that Lord Cornwallis preceded the troops and
paused briefly for food and shelter at this tavern.

Continue a short distance further on the path to a
monument marking the place where Cornwallis's men
began their ascent of the steep cliff. Then proceed on the
cobbled road up the hill and turn left at the fork. The trail
ascends through woods of hemlock, sugar maple, tulip

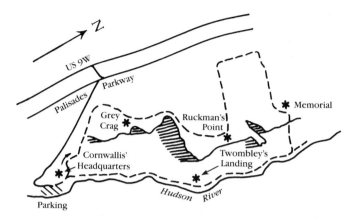

trees, and black birch. All but the tulip tree are more typical of northern than southern forests, and they grow here because the ravine affords them a cool, moist refuge from the drier ridge tops above.

The trail here and in many other places is flanked by poison ivy; be careful! When you come to a stone archway, bear right onto the blue-blazed path. Shortly the trail meets the entrance road and follows it past park headquarters, then reenters the woods 100 yards further on the right. The woods along here are predominantly maple with scattered pine, beech, and sweet gum.

Notice how the exposed rock on this section of the trail is quite smooth. This is the result of polishing by fine rock fragments dragged across the Palisades ridge by the Wisconsin glacier. The glacier also carved scratches, known as striations, into the rock along the Palisades ridge, and these can also be seen along this part of the trail.

A short distance further, a side trail leads to the right. Follow this along the edge of a deep, narrow canyon and over a cement bridge to an overlook. You are now standing on the largest section of separated rock in the Palisades: Grey Crag. The crag is some 300 feet long and 10 to 20 feet wide. Here is a good place to view the Palisades up close. The many-sided columns you see were formed by huge vertical fissures in the rock, which were produced as the magma cooled and contracted. Horizontal cracks often intersect these vertical fissures, with the result that the diabase rock tends to break down into distinct masses that resemble stairs. This resemblance has led to calling this and other formations of intruded igneous rock traprock, a term derived from the Swedish "trapp," meaning stairs.

Retrace your steps to the trail and make another detour to the right just before crossing a footbridge to reach another overlook. Hemlocks squeeze their way out of the rock ledge here. In winter, both the hemlocks and the ledge are occasionally draped with snow or ice, the ice sometimes hanging in long columns formed by small cascades.

You will soon cross the creek again and follow the trail through a hemlock grove. Partridgeberry, a delicate, evergreen, trailing plant with small heart-shaped leaves, is one of the few plants that can survive the acid soil conditions beneath the hemlocks. Here and elsewhere on the trail it is the most conspicuous herb.

The trail eventually swings to the right over a footbridge built of fractured rock and through an area of gray birch and staghorn sumac. Staghorn sumac is a tall shrub bearing long, compound leaves with eleven to thirty-one sharply toothed leaflets. The young branches and leaf stalks are densely covered with soft hairs, giving them a velvety appearance. The presence of gray birch and staghorn sumac indicates some type of disturbance, and closer inspection will reveal that the area has experienced a fire in the relatively recent past. A side trail leads to a nice overlook, where gulls can often be seen gliding effortlessly above the river. In the fall, if one is lucky, a peregrine falcon may be seen passing these cliffs during its migration

Cornwallis Headquarters, Palisades Interstate Park

south. These magnificent birds formerly nested on ledges along the Palisades, until their near extinction from the effects of pesticides. It is hoped that captive-bred peregrines will someday have eyries here again.

The trail ends abruptly at Ruckman's Point, where there is a small clearing bounded by a concrete wall; the cliff here is 520 feet high. This is one of the many "pitching places" along the Palisades, where wood cut from the ridgetop forest was pitched over the cliff. Below were usually smooth or small-stone talus slopes where the wood would not smash or wedge upon landing. Originally, these forests supplied fuel to the Hudson River steamboats, then later for the home-heating needs of wealthy New Yorkers, who bought up sections of the cliffs for just this purpose.

Follow the grassy path (Ruckman's Road) away from the cliff and then swing right into the woods. The trail passes a series of clefts in the rock. Look carefully along the left for a trail that leads over these clefts. About ¹/₂ mile further it reaches the New Jersey State Federation of Women's Clubs Memorial. The federation was instrumental in getting the

Cliffs at Ruckman's Point, Palisades Interstate Park

enabling legislation passed that resulted in the creation of the Palisades Interstate Park Commission in 1900.

The impetus for the creation of such a commission was the destruction of the cliffs by commercial quarrying in the 1800s. The traprock cliffs were blasted to supply ship's ballast in the middle of the century, then later for building material for Manhattan roads and buildings. A large quarry in the Palisades at Haverstraw, New York, still supplies this valuable rock for a variety of commercial uses. One can usually see barges from this quarry bearing the name New York Trap Rock Company being towed along the Hudson River.

The trail reenters the woods behind the monument and continues as a blue-and-white-blazed trail. At a fork, bear right to follow a steep series of steps down to the River Trail. At the bottom, turn left for a short distance and stop just before a stand of white birch trees, which are seldom seen this far south. From here look up to Ruckman's Point (south) and Indian Head to the north. The Indian head formed by the crags looks more like a stoic Yankee settler from this vista.

Retrace your steps past the ascending path and follow the white-blazed shore path. Most of the trees at the base of the talus slopes along here are black locusts, recognized by their delicate compound leaves and thorned branches. Scattered among the locusts are Princess-trees, which were imported from Asia for the old estate gardens along where the Palisades Parkway now lies. The clusters of large purple flowers appear in May.

In about 3/4 mile, the trail emerges onto a grassy area known as Twombley's Landing. Oyster shell middens found here indicate that this is the site of a former Indian camp. A quarter of a mile further the trail forks, the right fork leading along the base of the cliff, while the left fork leads along the shore past the remains of Excelsior Dock. The trails rejoin and 1/2 mile further the parking area is reached.

10. Great Falls/S.U.M. Historic District

Distance: 2 miles (Easy)
Walking time: 2 hours
Directions: From the east, take Interstate 80 west to the Paterson Main St. exit, then go left 2 blocks to Grand St. Turn left and go 4 blocks to Spruce St. From the west, take the Central Business District exit which loops under I-80 to Grand St. Turn left and go one block to Spruce St. Turn right, go 3 blocks to McBride Ave. exit, and turn right again. Park at Haines Overlook Park, which is immediately on the left. (201) 279-9587

Paterson has been called "the cradle of American industry." Here the cotton industry developed the cotton-duck sail, the locomotive industry produced a significant portion of the nation's locomotives, the world's leading silk manufacturing center was founded, the first submarine was invented, and the Colt revolver and Wright's airplane engines were manufactured. Most of these early industries depended on the Great Falls—a 280-foot-wide waterfall which plunges nearly 80 feet through a narrow gorge—for their power. Harnessed by a unique group of American entrepreneurs, this inexpensive and abundant source of energy brought Paterson to national prominence during the nineteenth century.

By the early twentieth century, labor unrest and an exodus of industry to the south removed Paterson from the forefront of American industry, but much of the city's rich engineering, industrial, and architectural heritage can be seen today in the Great Falls of the Passaic/S.U.M. Historic District.

From the parking lot, you can see the Great Falls straight ahead, framed by massive cliffs of basalt. This basalt was formed about 200 million years ago during the late Triassic

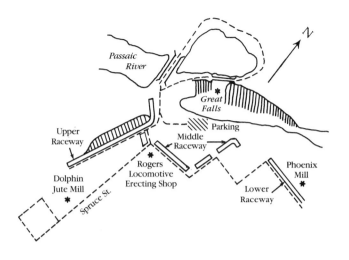

period, when large amounts of lava poured out from rifts caused by stress deep beneath the earth's surface. The lava cooled quickly and was later covered by sediments, but was uncovered again when the basin in which Paterson now lies was tilted. This tilting caused rapid erosion of the softer sedimentary rock around the solidified lava, leaving it as a basaltic ridge known as the first Watchung Mountain.

At this particular point along the first Watchung Mountain, the ridge is traversed by the Passaic River, which passes through a narrow gorge that is the result of collapse of the basalt along weak zones in the jointed rock. Huge sections of rock that have fallen away from the cliffs can be seen lying at the base of the falls. (Remember that the falls are most spectacular after a heavy rain.)

Next to the overlook area is a statue of Alexander Hamilton, who first envisioned the falls as a source of power for industry. As secretary of the treasury during the late 1700s, Hamilton tried to involve the government in developing a planned industrial city around the Great Falls.

Congress rejected the idea, but Hamilton succeeded in encouraging a group of prominent businessmen to undertake the planning and operating of such a city. In 1791, the group incorporated as the Society for the Establishment of Useful Manufactures (S.U.M.), a corporation that was to shape Paterson's growth for more than 150 years.

From the overlook, walk back toward McBride Avenue, turn right, and follow Spruce Street to the path that leads to the bridge across the Great Falls. (In winter, the gate may be closed, as beautiful but treacherous layers of ice are formed on the bridge.) Below lies the S.U.M. Hydroelectric Generating Plant, man's most recent effort at harnessing the power of the Great Falls. The S.U.M. built the plant in 1914 to produce energy for the mills nearby, its four huge turbines generating 21 million kilowatts per year. Though it has been closed since 1969, the city hopes to reactivate the plant, which could provide thousands of homes and factories with electricity.

After crossing the footbridge, swing left along the edge of the falls. This is a good place to see how the basalt cliff has broken up into a series of narrow chasms. The remains of an early stone dam that crossed the river can be seen from here also. You then pass the Passaic Valley Water Commission and Testing Station and the S.U.M. Conduit House before turning left. This path passes the remains of the S.U.M. Steam Plant, built in 1876, and follows along Maple Street for a short distance.

The path swings left to run parallel to the bank of the pool above the falls and then joins Wayne Avenue. Turn left and follow this road over the river—upstream can be seen the concrete dam built in 1838 to supply water to the S.U.M. raceway—and then turn right onto Spruce Street. Immediately on the right is a gate which opens onto a footpath along the upper raceway; go through this gate and follow the path. The raceway, built between 1828 and 1846, drew water from the Passaic and supplied it to the mills via spillways and wooden flumes. Near the entrance to the raceway on the left can be seen the spillway that fed the wheelhouse of the Ivanhoe Paper Mill. The wheelhouse, built in 1865, housed an 87-inch turbine that supplied power to a complex of ten buildings where paper was manufactured from rags. These buildings are gone now, but the wheelhouse itself still stands.

Follow the raceway to the end; here a spillway used to lead down to the middle raceway, which can be seen below. Next to the spillway is a mulberry tree, identified by its heart-shaped, fine-toothed leaves which are often lobed. The mulberry was introduced from Asia in an attempt to feed silkworms for the silk industry. The attempt was unsuccessful, however, and Paterson's silk mills were forced to import raw silk from China and Japan.

Continue back on the lower path along the raceway and turn right onto Spruce Street. Along the right side of the street are a number of large mills. The Barbour flax Company made linen thread and twine beginning in 1865, while the Dolphin Jute Company, established in 1844, converted hemp and jute into twine, rope, and carpet backing. One of Paterson's largest mills, the Dolphin Company encompassed seventeen buildings.

Just past the Dolphin Jute Mill, now the Great Falls Industrial Park, turn right onto Barbour Street and follow it out to Grand Street. Barbour Street is paved with cobblestone, as once many of Paterson's streets were, and one can easily imagine the sound of carts carrying goods from the mills rolling along this street. At Grand Street turn left and then left again to return to Spruce Street.

Down the street 1 1/2 blocks on the right is the Rogers Locomotive Erecting Shop, built in 1835, and rebuilt in 1871. The eighty-ton locomotives constructed here began as small parts on the top floor and were put together in stages, each larger assembly gradually moving down toward the main floor. The completed engines then rolled through the massive wooden doors that face the street. Rogers and five other Paterson locomotive manufacturers

Great Falls of the Passaic River, Paterson

together built nearly one-fourth of all the nineteenth-century steam engines in America.

Many Paterson steam locomotives were shipped overseas, including 144 of the 246 American locomotives used to build the Panama Canal. One of those was Old 299, which returned to Paterson in 1979 and can be seen at the rear of the Rogers Locomotive Erecting Shop. The Rogers building itself has been restored and currently houses an exhibit on the history of industry in Paterson.

From the Rogers building, continue down Spruce Street past the Union Works/Rosen Mill. Constructed in 1890 as a locomotive manufacturing plant, the building was converted to ribbon manufacturing in 1916. Just past the Union Works, the middle section of the S.U.M. raceway system leads to the right; follow the path along the raceway to where it meets McBride Avenue. Work on the original raceway system began in 1792, when the newly formed Society for the Establishment of Useful Manufactures hired Pierre L'Enfant, the French architect-engineer who designed Washington, D.C., to design a system that would channel water for power to mills constructed and operated by the S.U.M. L'Enfant left Paterson in 1793 because of differences of opinion with the S.U.M., but the raceway was finally completed in 1838, first under Peter Colt's direction, and then under that of his son Roswell.

As the raceway emerges at McBride Avenue, look across the street and to the left. The reddish rock that is exposed here is Brunswick formation sandstone, formed in Triassic times before the volcanic episodes that created the Watchung Mountains occurred. Like the sandstone of the Stockton formation found to the south, the sandstone here was quarried for use as building stone, especially during the nineteenth century. At that time, much of the quarried stone found its way into Paterson's buildings, and also into the raceway canals, which are lined with locally quarried brownstone.

Directly above the layers of sandstone can be seen the Watchung basalt, which is brownish in color in some places because of the weathering of iron-bearing minerals in the rock. Like the brownstone, basalt was also quarried to serve Paterson's industries. The pinnacle of basalt to the left of this outcrop (near the Haines Overlook Park) marks the former height of a basalt ridge, which was quarried away before the early 1900s.

Turn right onto McBride Avenue and follow it downhill to Mill Street and turn left. After passing the Franklin Mill and Essex Mill (on the left), the road bends right. The raceway emerges again here, and beyond it lies what remains of one of Paterson's most famous industries—the Colt Gun Mill. This two-story building to the left of the smokestack originally towered four stories and was topped by a six-story cupola bell tower. Here Samuel Colt built his first production firearms, and between 1836 and 1841,

Great Falls/S.U.M. Historic District 79

approximately 5,000 muskets, rifles, and revolvers were made here. This building and the crumbling Waverly Mill on the right are scheduled for restoration in the near future.

Swing right to follow the raceway along Van Houten Street, passing the Todd Mill and the Nightingale Mill before coming to the Phoenix Mill complex at number 15^1/$_2$. The Phoenix Mill was operating as early as 1815, producing candlewick and cotton, later switching to linen and flax production. In 1860, Benjamin Tilt began silk production on the top floor of the factory, and by 1865 he controlled the entire structure, converting it from cotton production to silk. In the 1880s, the Phoenix Company employed 8,000 people and had 500 looms. Altogether in Paterson there were 120 silk mills with nearly 15,000 workers, producing half of the silk in the United States.

It was about this same time that the workers in the silk mills began to organize for better pay and working conditions. In 1913, organized by the Industrial Workers of the World, over 20,000 silk workers staged an industry-wide strike. During the strike the I.W.W. leaders used to meet in a bar across the street from the Phoenix Mill; this building survives as the Question Mark Bar.

The strike in some ways marked the ebbing of Paterson's industrial growth, growth that had lasted over a century and a half and had produced a variety of industrial achievements. As you return to the parking lot (backtrack along Van Houten Street and then McBride Avenue), consider that these achievements, though notable, did not come without some severe damage to the environment. The devastated traprock cliffs, the fouled waters of the Passaic, and the smoke-filled air are as much reminders of what is destructive about our use of the environment as the graceful brick and brownstone buildings are of our constructive endeavors.

11. Morristown National Historical Park

Jockey Hollow Area
Distance: 3 miles (Moderate)
Walking time: 1½ hours
Directions: From the north, take Interstate 287 to exit 26B (marked Bernardsville and US 202); from the south, take 287 to the second Maple Ave. exit (marked N. Maple Ave. and US 202), following signs to Jockey Hollow. Then turn right at the traffic light and go north on US 202, 1.8 miles to Tempe Wick Rd. and turn left. The entrance to the park is 1½ miles ahead on the right. Park in the main parking lot in front of the visitor's center. The park is open 8:00 A.M. to 5:00 P.M. every day except Thanksgiving Day and New Year's Day. (201) 235-0353

When George Washington led the Continental Army into winter quarters in Morristown in 1777, he could not have chosen a better place to rest and reassemble his army, which was weary from hard-won battles at Trenton and Princeton. From the prosperous farms nearby, wheat, corn, oats, vegetables, and fruits were available. Much of the land was forested and could supply firewood and timber for huts. Nearby creeks provided ample fresh water. Mines and furnaces to the north supplied iron to be worked into tools and weapons. A mill on the Whippany River was a ready source of gunpowder made from saltpeter, sulfur, and charcoal.

The most important resources that were provided by the land around Morristown were the Watchung Mountains east of town. This double ridge of massive basalt formed natural ramparts whose passes could be easily defended. Lookouts posted on ridge tops could readily detect any movement by the British, who were camped in New York City, thirty miles away. Confident that the enemy could

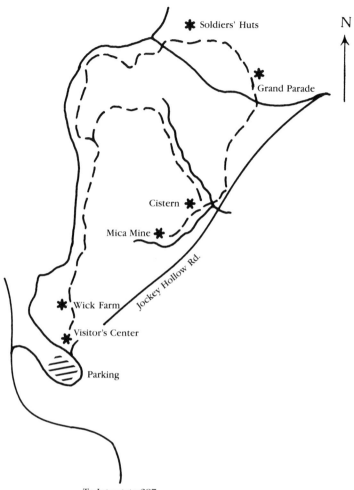

N

Soldiers' Huts

Grand Parade

Cistern

Mica Mine

Jockey Hollow Rd.

Wick Farm

Visitor's Center

Parking

To Interstate 287

not attack, Washington used Morristown as a rallying place, in the winter of both 1777 and 1779.

The encampments of the Continental Army were located about four miles south of Morristown in Jockey Hollow. Nearly 1,000 acres of land here are preserved as part of the Morristown National Historical Park. The area today looks much as it did when the Continental Army arrived there in the winter of 1777. This walk tells the story of that army as it struggled to survive.

Begin at the visitor's center, where one can obtain trail maps and other information. The trail maps are not displayed, but can be requested from the interpreter at the center. Before leaving the visitor's center be sure to look at the mural depicting the encampment.

Follow the gravel path to the Wick Farm. Though the Wick Farm has been restored because of its role in American military history (the house served as Gen. Arthur St. Clair's headquarters during the 1779–1780 encampment), its richness lies in the glimpse it provides us of a prosperous family of that day. By 1780, the farm included 1,400 acres, most of it woodland, which provided lumber and firewood. The cleared acreage yielded a wide variety of products to meet the family's needs: cereals, fruits, vegetables, and livestock.

Look out over the well-kept orchard and imagine children harvesting apples in October. The herb garden next to the house has well-labeled plants that give an idea of how Mrs. Wick would have livened up a ham or turkey. Passing the barn in back, one is reminded of the winter of 1779, when not a few of Henry Wick's sheep, geese, and pigs were pilfered by the starving soldiers of the Continental Army.

Continue past the barn and turn right onto the paved road. Just past the fork, look for a trail marker and map posted on the right. The trail leading into the woods takes you through a young deciduous wood predominantly of white ash and black locust, with some stands of beech. It

Restored Revolutionary War soldiers' cabins, Morristown
National Historical Park

is interesting to note that in describing the cutting of these
same woods in 1779, officers and soldiers referred to the
woods as being of "oak, chestnut, and walnut." Today, no
mature chestnuts can be found because of the blight that
eliminated them earlier in this century. However, what has
become of the oak and walnut?

The walnuts the soldiers wrote about were really
hickory trees of three species: pignut, mockernut, and
shagbark. Almost all of the early settlers used the term
walnut to describe the hickories. The oaks referred to
were indeed oaks, most likely white, red, and scarlet oaks,
but both the oaks and hickories are poorly represented in
the contemporary forest cover.

The forest here is actually in a rather early stage of

succession which will eventually lead back to the type of forest described by the Continental soldiers. After these woods had been cut to supply the soldiers' needs, they began to return, only to be cut repeatedly in the 1800s to produce charcoal. Now that this land is protected from this type of human disturbance, the white ash and black locust that are presently so common will eventually yield to oaks and hickories.

An interesting change in the wildlife associated with these forests accompanies this forest transition. Woodpeckers are not as numerous in these woods today as they will be when a mature forest containing more dead trees provides better feeding and nesting sites. Mammals will profit from mature trees also. The hollow centers the trees develop as they age will provide shelter for gray squirrels, flying squirrels, raccoons, and opossums.

One-half mile from the start, the trail comes to an intersection. Bear left on the trail to the soldier huts that skirts the edge of a small ravine and then turns right to parallel the paved road and a stream. Notice how many of the young ash and locust trees are covered with grape and poison ivy vines struggling to get their share of the sunlight. Another $^1/_2$ mile further, the trail emerges into a grassy area. In front of you is the hillside where over 200 log huts once stood. The soldiers constructed these huts themselves, as well as the bunks, tables, and chairs that furnished them. Each hut measured fourteen by sixteen feet, was six and one-half feet high, and housed twelve men. Log chimneys covered with plaster rose up from fireplaces built of stone. Fueled by locally cut timber, the fires in these hearths cooked the soldiers' food and provided them with a minimal amount of warmth.

After inspecting the huts, follow the trail to the right from the lone hut in the back up to an interpretive sign that describes the encampments, which have long since disappeared, having been reclaimed by the woods. All that remains are the stone hearths, which can be found

Apple orchard, Morristown National Historical Park

scattered throughout the area. One of these hearths lies a few feet to the right of the interpretive sign. Go left from the sign, and then turn right at the T at the top of the hill. The red and yellow blazes you see on the trees here are part of a gypsy-moth control experiment being conducted by the New Jersey Department of Agriculture.

At the next T, go right again and watch your footing as you descend the hill. Huge tulip trees dot the slope here. In May and June, the large tuliplike orange flowers are conspicuous. These flowers give way to artichokelike fruits, which in winter provide food for gray squirrels, purple finches, and evening grosbeaks. Below the tulip trees, spicebush becomes common; its yellow flowers bloom early in spring.

Shortly the trail emerges onto an open field known as the Grand Parade. Cross over to the right where there are a number of interpretive displays. This quiet meadow once rang with the sounds of military drills. Inspections took place here almost daily. Here, guards received their assignments, offenders were punished, and the troops heard general orders. Occasionally military displays were conducted here for Washington's guests, as when Lafayette came to Morristown.

Cross the road and turn onto the fire trail and follow this $1/4$ mile to a parking area. Follow along the back of the lot to the sign saying Aqueduct Trail and reenter the woods. After crossing a small wooden-plank bridge over a stream, turn right on the fire road (marked by an iron gate). Then, where the road forks, go left. The trail here becomes flanked by Christmas fern and a small stream. This stream is one of those that supplied the Continental Army with water during the encampment. Almost a century later, this and other streams in Jockey Hollow were impounded to supply water to the growing village of Morristown. The trail comes upon an old brick cistern which was part of these waterworks.

For an interesting detour, continue along the stream for about $1/4$ mile. The rubble along the left of the trail is actually the remains of one of the waterworks impoundments. When the trail comes to a low hill of jumbled rock, stop and take a closer look. These rocks are tailings from a mica mine which was worked during the 1800s. Before glass came into use, mica sheets, called isinglass, were used as windows.

Retrace your steps to the cistern, and follow the trail back to the fire road and turn left. This road leads you back to the trail to the Wick Farm, the start of your walk.

12. Lord Stirling Park

The Edge of the Great Swamp
Distance: 3^1/$_2$ miles (Easy)
Walking time: 2^1/$_2$ hours
Directions: Take Interstate 287 to exit 26 (marked N.
Maple Ave. and Basking Ridge). Follow Maple Ave. 2^1/$_2$
miles. Turn left onto Lord Stirling Rd. and go 1 mile. Look
for the Environmental Education Center on left. The center
and trails are open 9 A.M. to 5:00 P.M. daily. (908) 766-2489

An extensive boardwalk system, observation towers and
blinds, and an attractive visitor's center make this walk
unique. The area, Lord Stirling Park, is administered by the
Somerset County Park Commission, which has built almost
12,000 feet of six-foot-wide boardwalk and many wooden
bridges to make it easy to penetrate the inaccessible Great
Swamp basin. The park gets its name from colonial times
when the land was a small part of the vast holdings of
William Alexander, the lord of Stirling, who served as a
general in the Continental Army.

Lord Stirling Park lies on the western edge of the Great
Swamp basin. The basin is the remnant of Glacial Lake
Passaic, which formed approximately 12,000 years ago
when water from the melting glacier became trapped
between the retreating Wisconsin ice sheet to the north,
and the Watchung Mountains to the south and east. Layer
upon layer of clay sediments were laid down at the bottom
of this glacial lake, making the soil impervious to water
and thus preventing drainage. As the ice sheet retreated
further, a gap near what is today Paterson was uncorked,
allowing the waters to flow out, creating a series of low-
lying minilakes. However, because of the topography and
the impervious clay soil, these minilakes never drained
completely, but like lakes everywhere slowly filled in with
silt and organic matter.

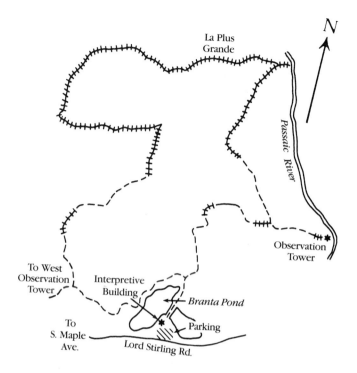

La Plus
Grande

Passaic River

Observation
Tower

To West
Observation
Tower

Interpretive
Building

Branta Pond

To
S. Maple
Ave.

Parking

Lord Stirling Rd.

Before starting your walk, stop at the Education Center,
which houses a library, an exhibit hall, and a book and gift
shop. Before you leave the building, you might ask at the
desk about the day's trail conditions. Despite the extensive
boardwalk, portions of the trail can be quite soggy at
times.

Follow the red trail (marked by colored reflectors) over
Branta Pond, a man-made pond which serves as home to
many muskrat and Canada geese. Note the "island" at the
center of the pond where a small weather station is
located. In the fields to the right of the trail here can be
seen a variety of birds that prefer this type of habitat:
eastern kingbirds, brown thrashers, meadowlarks, field
sparrows, and occasionally, bluebirds.

Lord Stirling Park 89

Stay on the red trail; soon you cross two wooden bridges. This area is dominated by red maple, which is a common woody pioneer in the swamp forest. Before long, the woods become denser, the maples and scattered gray birch giving way to white oak, black birch, and some beech trees. This is one of the areas in which the water table is slightly further below the surface and the soil is consequently drier. Another tree characteristic of these drier pockets appears here also: the shagbark hickory, easily recognized by its light-colored bark flaking in long, loose strips.

At the T following the second section of boardwalk, turn right to follow the unmarked trail to the observation tower. Continue to a T and turn right, where you emerge into an open field full of goldenrod and occasional hawthorns. The hawthorns make this field excellent winter habitat for northern shrikes, also known as butcher birds. These birds have no talons, and so they impale their prey on a barbed-wire fence or sharp thorn such as that of the hawthorn, to make it easier to tear it apart. Small birds and rodents are their usual prey, and if you look sharply, you may find one impaled on these thorns during the fall or winter. This field and the others in the park are visible reminders that the area was farmed at one time—up until the late 1950s, in fact.

Take the mowed path into the field and on the far side turn left and follow it to a boardwalk that reenters the woods. The observation tower here looks east across the Passaic River, which is the principal drainage for the Great Swamp basin. The river is flanked by willows, ash, and red maple, with reed grass and cattails on the floodplain beyond. In summer, the pink and white blossoms of swamp rose mallow make this a lovely spot. Spend a few minutes looking for American bitterns and other herons before retracing your steps.

Follow the mowed path back through the center of the field, turn right at the T, and continue straight instead of returning to the boardwalk crossed earlier. As you pass a large standing chestnut hulk on the right, notice the foliage at the top. This may at first appear to be a final attempt at growth by this venerable tree, but the foliage really belongs to a less venerable plant—poison ivy. The thick vine can be seen leading from the base of the tree.

The trail then skirts the edge of a marsh that is drying out and becomes a boardwalk again. The boardwalk crosses a series of rivulets lined with arrowhead and pickerelweed and then passes some thickets of red osier and silky dogwood and arrowwood. Two species of skullcaps—marsh and mad dog—which are violet-flowered members of the mint family, are common along here. The curious parasitic plant—dodder—also grows here. Lacking any green leaves, its orange stems look like a mass of tangled fishing line.

Bearing right at the fork, follow the trail back to the river for one more look. Be especially sure to take this look in August when the scarlet of cardinal flowers brightens the river bank. Turn around and follow the boardwalk to the right, away from the river, and emerge into La Plus Grande, a magnificent area of open water ringed by a lovely freshwater marsh. Broad- and narrow-leaved cattails yield to plants such as meadowsweet, willow, and swamp rose. Buttonbush, a semiaquatic shrub whose small white flowers are clustered in ball-like heads, is abundant here also. Its blossoms are visited by scores of nectar-seeking bees and butterflies in mid-summer.

At your feet are a number of interesting plants also. Arrowhead and its smaller-flowered relative water plantain, ground nut, and wild mint all grow along the boardwalk here. In the thickets nearby can be seen catbirds, cedar waxwings, and long-billed marsh wrens. Green herons and great blue herons stalk fish and frogs in the waters, and at dusk in August one can pause to watch dozens of night-hawks winging their way overhead. Turn right at the fork where the trail passes briefly through a wooded area.

Boardwalk, Lord Stirling Park

After leaving La Plus Grande, the boardwalk enters different woods from what has been seen so far. Pin oak is the main tree here, with a lower layer of ironwood, and below this are blueberry bushes. Ironwood, also known as hornbeam or musclewood, has distinctive smooth gray bark which is stretched over a muscular-looking trunk. This small tree is a common member of the understory in areas with moist, rich soil. The ground underneath the ironwood is covered with hummocks of sedge. Continue through these woods to a fork in the boardwalk and go right. Great crested flycatchers can often be heard overhead along this part of the trail. Along the ground, ovenbirds and occasional thrushes are heard.

Just after this section of boardwalk ends, the gravel path leads past an American beech tree on the left lying parallel to the ground, forming a natural bench. This tree was struck by lightning ten years ago, and while part of the main trunk is dead, new vertical branches have grown up on each end. The air around a bolt of lightning is heated to such a high temperature that a struck tree is actually blown apart by the force of the expanding water vapor inside the tree. Occasionally, bits of charred lichen, fungus, and bark can he found near the struck tree.

Just beyond this tree, go right on the gravel path and then bear right at the fork just before a marshy area known as Woodpecker Swamp. Bear left at the next fork, from where the trail leads onto a boardwalk again and soon comes to a huge white oak along the left of the trail. This oak is probably over 300 years old. A forester would call it a wolf tree—typically a large, short-trunked, spreading tree that "wolfs" more than its share of the light from the canopy overhead. Such trees grow in open areas, and this one gives evidence that the area around it may have been open pastureland for many years.

Continue on the red trail to where an unmarked trail joins it from the left. To the left of the trail near here is an area where many small depressions in the soil can be seen. These were created when the previous owners of the land sold live trees to be used in landscaping the 1965 World's Fair grounds in New York. The trees were selected because the high water table in this area causes the roots to grow close to the surface, making the trees easier to remove.

Continue on the red trail past Bridge 5 and bear right onto the unmarked trail. This trail leads through an abandoned field ringed by goldenrod and staghorn sumac, and passes a small semipermanent pond on the right, now largely overgrown with cattails. If you look closely to the left of the pond, you can see traces of the reddish rock that lines the bottom of the pond and that underlies all of the Great Swamp basin: soft shale and sandstone, which are brownish red in color. The sediments that make up this rock were deposited about 190 million years ago during the period when dinosaurs roamed this area. This rock was of importance to New York City and other eastern cities in the late 1800s, as it was quarried for building stones. The brownstone of Manhattan's and Brooklyn's brownstone houses is actually red sandstone quarried in this area.

Continue through the field, bearing right at the fork. Late summer flowers along here include wild bergamot and dense blazing star. Stop at the observation tower and look out over the fields you have just walked through. Woodchucks and cottontail rabbits can frequently be seen here. Kingbirds sally out from perches in the field to snap up flying insects, and the "wicker" call of the flicker is heard as it scratches about looking for ants.

Retrace your steps down the hill from the tower to the fork by the pond and turn right. Where this mowed path passes through a small section of trees, go left on another path leading through the field. On the far side, turn left to meet the red trail again, take it to the right, and follow it to the blind on the edge of Branta Pond. Canada geese and wood ducks are most frequently seen on the pond; from this blind they can be easily observed at close range. From here, follow the red trail to the right and back to the Environmental Education Center.

13. Herrontown Woods

Distance: 1¹/₄ miles (Easy)
Walking time: 2 hours
Directions: From the north, take NJ 27 to Princeton, from
the south US 206. (Both of these roads lead into Nassau St.
in downtown Princeton.) Turn right off Nassau St. 1¹/₄
miles northeast of the center of town (left if coming from
the south) onto Snowden Lane and follow the signs to
Herrontown Woods. The area is open 8:00 A.M. to 5:00 P.M.
from November to April, 8:00 A.M. to 8:00 P.M. from May to
October.

The forest of Herrontown Woods, like all forests, is a
product of a variety of environmental factors such as soil
type, topography, and geology. In addition, as with so
much of New Jersey's landscape, the patterns of the
contemporary forest have their origins in changes wrought
by man's use of the land. Herrontown Woods, though
unspectacular, is an excellent place to gain a better
understanding of how these factors interact, as the mosaic
of forest types found here occurs in a small area.

Begin your walk at the red-blazed trail near the entrance
to the parking lot. (There is a trail map posted next to the
trail entrance.) This trail immediately passes through a
number of red pines and then shortly emerges to turn
right across an old stone wall. The young woods along this
part of the trail are mainly made up of white ash and red
maple, two of the most important pioneers to invade
abandoned land in the New Jersey Piedmont. Both the red
pines and the young forest here are growing on farmland
abandoned around the turn of the century; the stone walls
attest to the fact that this land was formerly a hayfield or
pasture.

The trail emerges into a clearing where a cottage and

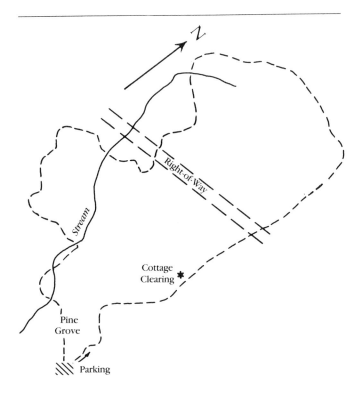

small barn are further remnants of the once active farm. Take the blue-blazed trail which leaves from the back of the clearing next to another wooden trail map. The soil along this portion of the trail is noticeably more moist than in the previous section, and the moist conditions allow many of the trees to reach fairly large size. The dominant trees are oaks—mainly white, black, and red—although they are joined occasionally by hickories and tulip trees. Below this mature forest canopy grow flowering dogwood and ironwood, and below these there is a shrub layer of spicebush, which thrives in the deep, moist soil.

A variety of wildflowers can be seen on the floor of this mature forest in early spring. Many of these plants do most of their growing and flowering before the canopy leaves out and makes the forest floor too dark for active growth. One of the earliest of these spring wildflowers is the spring beauty. It bears two grasslike leaves and a cluster of flower buds arranged in a "fiddlehead." The pink or white five-petaled flowers bloom sequentially, each flower lasting just one day Another common wildflower is Solomon's seal, which is recognized by its large, curved, single stem with smooth, oval leaves arranged alternately along it. Solomon's seal's yellowish, bell-shaped flowers appear in May, growing in pairs from the axils of the leaves. May-apple, skunk cabbage, jack-in-the-pulpit, and other wild-flowers preferring moist sites are also seen here in the spring.

As the trail begins to climb, the soil and the overlying vegetation can be seen to change dramatically. The wet spots that allowed plants like mayapple and skunk cabbage to thrive on the lower slope are no longer present, and the more drought-tolerant maple-leaf viburnum replaces the moisture-loving spicebush as the dominant shrub. Over-head, ironwood has dropped from the understory, and sweet gum and tulip tree have disappeared from the canopy. The large boulders scattered through the woods suggest the stoniness of the underlying soil.

These dark gray, angular boulders are a clue to the nature of the ridge that the trail has been ascending. The boulders are pieces of diabase, the rock that lies beneath all but the southeast corner of Herrontown Woods. Like the other volcanic rocks that are found in the Piedmont of New Jersey, this diabase was formed in late Triassic times, when volcanic activity forced great flows of molten rock up through the surrounding layers of sandstone and shale. This molten rock cooled slowly beneath the earth's surface, and did not become exposed until much later, after millions of years of erosion had stripped away the soft sedimentary rock, leaving the diabase as a ridge. The diabase ridge here at Herrontown Woods is known as Rocky Hill, but it is geologically part of the same sill (an intrusive rock that follows parallel to the beds of the intruded layers of rock), that forms the Palisades along the Hudson River.

The trail comes out to a swath cut through the woods for a gas pipeline right-of-way, then reenters the woods again. To the left of the trail here can be seen evidence of an old traprock quarry, marked by angular blocks of diabase with small excavations in front of them. Closer inspection of the diabase outcrops will reveal evidence of the quarrying: the straight, narrow grooves on the face of the outcrops are marks caused by a star drill, which was used by quarrymen to fracture the rock. In the late nineteenth century, diabase was removed from quarries all along this ridge to be used as crushed rock for road building and other purposes. Today, Trap Rock Industries, Inc., of Kingston still quarries diabase nearby for road materials and concrete aggregate. Dump trucks are seen constantly on the roads around Kingston, roaring to and from the quarry, picking up loads of traprock for construction projects.

The trail continues along the top of the diabase ridge, through an area where the trees are somewhat smaller and more closely spaced than on the slope below, indicating that it may have been cut more recently. Red, white, and black oaks again are the principal trees, but in some places pin oak is also seen. The leaf of the black oak has an oval outline, cut by two to three deep sinuses on each side. Each of the five to seven lobes of the black-oak leaf has several points. The black bark is ridged, with widely spaced furrows between the ridges. The red oak is similar to the black oak, but its leaves are not quite as stout, and its bark is gray with wide reddish furrows. Do not be disturbed if you find certain trees that are intermediate between the two species: these trees hybridize freely with one another, and their progeny hybridize occasionally also. This mixed oak forest soon yields to a "new" forest, however. Sweet gum becomes the dominant tree; this is

Jack-in-the-pulpit, Herrontown Woods

especially easy to observe in the fall, when the trail is littered with the fallen fruits. Growing with the sweet gum are black oaks, red maple, shagbark and pignut hickory, and below these grows a shrub layer of blackhaw, a relative of maple-leaf viburnum. Its egg-shaped, five-toothed leaves look much like those of the black cherry tree, but are distinguished by being oppositely arranged. Its blackish fruits, which are eaten by foxes, ruffed grouse, and occasionally by people, appear in early fall.

A small grove of beech trees is traversed before the trail reaches a very moist area near the headwaters of a small stream that drains this ridgetop. The red maple trees (often called swamp maples, suggesting their affinity for wet areas) that abound here are distinctive in that many have roots that protrude a few inches above the ground. Such adventitious roots occur often in areas where trees are seasonally inundated by water. The moistness of this area is also indicated by the reappearance of ironwood in the understory and spicebush as the main shrub.

The trail reaches a junction with the red-blazed trail; turn left onto this trail, which crosses the stream and in about $1/8$ mile emerges onto the pipeline right-of-way again. After the trail reenters the woods, turn right almost immediately onto a white-blazed trail. This trail leads downhill a short distance and then joins a yellow-blazed trail; turn right here.

At one point the trail skirts the edge of a huge traprock boulder that has fractured to form a concave seat in the face of the rock. In spring and summer, this is a good place to sit and rest for a few minutes, and to listen for bird songs. Two of the most common songs you're likely to hear are those of the wood thrush and the ovenbird. The wood thrush's song is one of the most beautiful of North American birdsongs; its rich, flutelike melody prompted Henry David Thoreau to write: "Whenever a man hears it he is young, and Nature is in her spring;

wherever he hears it, it is a new world and a free country, and the gates of heaven are not shut against him."

The ovenbird's song is less melodious than the wood thrush's, but it is equally distinctive. An emphatic "teacher, teacher, teacher" is repeated rapidly by the ovenbird in an insistent crescendo. The ovenbird, like the wood thrush, is more often heard than seen. Both are colored much like the leaf litter that carpets the forest floor, where they spend most of their time foraging quietly for insects. Despite these similarities, the two birds are quite different taxonomically, the wood thrush belonging to the thrush family, while the ovenbird (which gets its name from the domed, oven-shaped nest it builds on the ground), belongs to the wood warbler family.

The trail leads through a large boulder field and crosses the stream. Many of the oaks in this part of the woods— mainly red and black—are quite large, having perhaps been protected from the most recent logging by the steep slope and rocky terrain. This and other diabase and basalt ridges throughout New Jersey's Piedmont were important sources for firewood from the late eighteenth through the mid-nineteenth century, since almost all of the flatlands had been cleared for farming. The ridge that is now Herrontown Woods not only supplied fuel for farmers' stoves, but is said to have also been cut to provide fire-wood for some of the Princeton University faculty. Remember that in those days, everyone, farmer and academic alike, heated with wood.

The yellow trail eventually meets a green-blazed trail; turn right here. The trail has begun to level out somewhat, and this fact, combined with the reappearance of the stone walls, suggests that you have left the diabase ridge behind and emerged onto the low-lying, flatland of the Brunswick shale and sandstone. Careful observation along the streambed will confirm this, as pieces of reddish sedimentary rock can be seen. Many of the gray rocks that lie in the stream, though they appear like the volcanic rock diabase, are actually sedimentary in origin also. Being at the edge of the molten magma when it was intruded, some of the soft red shale in this area was baked to become the hard, gray rock seen here, called hornfels.

Continue following this trail across the stream and to the left. It again crosses the stream and leads to the parking lot, which is just beyond the plantation of white pines.

14. Charles Rogers Sanctuary and Princeton Institute Woods

Distance: 2 miles (Easy)
Walking time: 1 hour
Directions: Take US 1 to Princeton and exit at Alexander
St. Continue until you cross the Delaware and Raritan
Canal and take the first left, West Drive. Bear left at the
fork, then park on the right near the observation tower.

Because the Piedmont in New Jersey is so uniform topo-
graphically, its interest lies in other features of the landscape—its forests, animals, and bird life. On this walk,
many of these features are readily observed, as it begins at
a freshwater marsh, leads through a lovely riparian woodland, and concludes in a section of upland forest. In
spring, this diversity of habitat is attractive to northward
migrating birds, especially warblers, making these two
adjacent sanctuaries an excellent place to observe the
spring migration.

Before beginning your walk, make your way to the top
of the small observation tower that overlooks the marsh.
The principal plant here is the familiar cattail, followed by
pickerelweed, a stout plant with fleshy, arrowhead-shaped
leaves, which emerges from the shallower waters of the
marsh. Pickerelweed is easily recognized in summer by its
dense spike of violet blue flowers.

By late summer, the open waters of the marsh are
covered by duckweeds, a group of small green aquatic
plants. Common duckweed is by far the most abundant,
but it is joined here by at least two other species, including
the tiny, almost granular appearing *Wolffia*—the smallest
of all North American flowering plants. As their name
suggests, duckweeds are a favorite food of some surface-
feeding ducks, including mallards, blue-winged teal, and

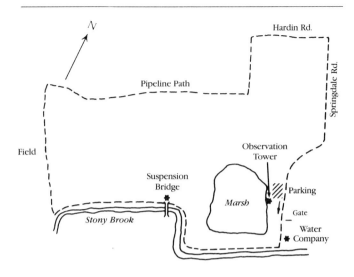

wood ducks, all of which are commonly seen on the marsh.

Along with the ducks, a variety of other animals can be seen on or above the marsh. Turtles sun themselves on tussock sedge hummocks, herons stalk frogs in the shallows, and redwing blackbirds sing "o-ka-reee" from the cattails. Overhead in fall, waves of blue jays, blackbirds, and other birds can be seen as they wing their way south.

From the observation tower, walk out to the road, turn right, and follow it to the Water Company parking lot. The trail enters the woods from the back right-hand corner of the lot. It follows along Stony Brook, while it is flanked on the right by the marsh. The forest here is made up of trees that thrive in the moist bottomland soil along the brook. Silver maples and box elder are two such trees. Box elder, also known as ash-leaf maple, is a small to medium-sized tree identified by its compound leaves, which usually bear three leaflets. In fall and winter, its fruit—the paired "keys" typical of the genus—identify it unmistakably as a maple.

Away from the brook, the most common tree is the pin

oak, a handsome tree which is familiar to many because of its frequent use in ornamental plantings. Pin oak is identified by its deeply cut, pointed leaves which resemble those of the scarlet oak, though they are somewhat smaller. The tree gets its name from the fact that some of its branches are usually stubby and pinlike. Also characteristic of the pin oak are its tangled lower branches, which typically point toward the ground.

The trail swings right along the brook, where it passes sweet-smelling spicebush and sinewy ironwood trees. A variety of herbaceous plants thrives in the wet soil below: spring beauty, mayapple, jack-in-the-pulpit, skunk cabbage, and others. In the fall, woodland asters of various species are conspicuous along the trail.

The damp alluvial soil of this bottomland forest is rich with earthworms, making it a likely place to see the American woodcock, which feeds almost exclusively on earthworms. The woodcock uses its long, prehensile bill to probe for, and then capture, the worms. This compact bird is magnificently camouflaged, and often permits close approach before exploding from the forest floor with whistling wings. In late March or early April, woodcocks are particularly conspicuous, not feeding here in the bottomland forest, but performing their elaborate courtship ritual on the edge of nearby fields. The male's loud nasal "peents" are followed by a spiraling takeoff and ascent, after which the bird swoops down to its takeoff point amid a series of strange warblings.

The trail bends to the left, passes a small suspension footbridge, and continues to follow the brook. Box elders lean out from the bank and occasional sycamores tower overhead. Hickories and ashes are also prominent in this riparian woodland. The ash found here is the green ash, identified by its tightly furrowed bark, its opposite twig arrangement, and its compound leaves bearing five to nine leaflets. It is very difficult to distinguish from the white ash, which is more common in upland areas. In spring, the

Stony Brook, Rogers Sanctuary

flowers of white ash appear before the leaves, while those of green ash appear after the leaf buds have opened; this is one way to tell the two apart where they do occur together.

Just before the trail bears right to follow the edge of a cornfield, it passes another common bottomland tree— the river birch. After the trail turns, however, the river birch, sycamores, box elders, and silver maples are left behind as the forest begins to include more upland species. Sweet gum, sassafras, and tulip trees are all common. Many of the trees are covered with vines, particularly wild grape, honeysuckle, and poison ivy. Another vine, found mainly along the small rivulets that drain toward Stony Brook, is the Canada moonseed. It is identified by its large, shallowly lobed leaves and its clusters of small white flowers, which develop into black fruits resembling wild grapes. These fruits should not be eaten, however, as they are mildly poisonous.

The trail soon reaches the pipeline right-of-way; turn right to follow this path. Just after you turn, you pass a catalpa tree on the left side of the trail. This tree's large heart-shaped leaves, showy white flowers, and long, slender fruit pods make it readily identifiable. A native of the Gulf Coast, the fast-growing catalpa was planted widely in the northeast for fence posts. Like many other alien plants, it has since escaped from cultivation, which accounts for its presence here.

In spring, the woods here are alive with warblers. These small, insectivorous birds tend to follow watercourses having a north-south orientation as they head north to their breeding grounds. Their northward migration through the riparian woodlands is "timed" to coincide with the hatching of the millions of caterpillars that feed voraciously on the green forest canopy. Redstarts, yellow-throated, cerulean, Cape May, Canada, chestnut-sided, black-throated blue, black-throated green, bay-breasted, blackburnian, blackpoll, black and white, and myrtle warblers—their names indicate the variety of these jewellike birds that can be seen here in the spring.

One of the migrating warblers that stays and makes its nest on the ground amid the sweet gums, tulip trees, and maples is the Kentucky warbler, which is near the edge of its range here. Because it forages close to the ground, the Kentucky warbler is difficult to see except when it betrays its presence by singing its loud "churree-churree-churree" song from a low perch.

Just past the intersection of the path with a foot trail, the woods change dramatically; the white pine and quaking aspen here suggest a relatively recent disturbance of the forest. Quaking aspen grows on all types of disturbed sites: clear-cut areas, burned land, and even along highways in the sterile mineral soil. It is recognized by its smooth chalk white to yellowish green bark, and by its small grayish green rounded leaves that "quake" in even the slightest breeze.

The path crosses a wide firebreak and then follows through a plantation of pine trees. The dry, needle-strewn

Cattails, Charles Rogers Sanctuary

floor of this pine plantation is a sharp contrast to the damp, thickly vegetated floor of the riparian woods traversed earlier. A short distance past the firebreak, a trail leads left into a small field. Walk straight through this field, past the red barn on the right, to the parking lot. On the left is a sign identifying the woods you have just passed through as belonging to the Institute for Advanced Study, a research institute composed of scholars from all over the world.

To return to your car, turn right onto Hardin Road, follow it to Springdale Road, and turn right, which leads you back to the parking area near the marsh. In the spring, the birding is excellent along this stretch of road.

The Delaware River Valley

Delaware River, near Stockton

15. Delaware and Raritan Canal State Park

Bull's Island
Distance: 2 $^1/_4$ miles (Easy)
Walking time: 1 $^1/_2$ hour
Directions: The park is located on NJ Highway 29, 3 miles north of Stockton. At the park entrance, cross the bridge over the canal and park in the lot just beyond the ranger's office. (908) 397-2949

Bull's Island is not really an island in the true geographical sense. It is, rather, a man-made island, created in the 1830s when the Delaware and Raritan Canal was built. Although not a true island, Bull's Island is distinctly different from the "mainland" nearby, since the Delaware and Raritan Canal sliced through the area where the floodplain forest of the Delaware River gives way to upland forest. This walk takes you under the canopy of a magnificent floodplain forest as well as out above a lovely stretch of the Delaware River.

From the parking lot, walk back toward the canal and turn right onto the footpath next to the fork in the entrance road; this path is well hidden, so look carefully. Long pants are recommended, since one of the plants that often encroaches upon the trail is the stinging nettle, whose coarse stinging hairs can cause painful irritation. The plant is most easily recognized by these hairs, which cover both the hollow stem and the coarsely toothed, heart-shaped leaves. In summer, the stinging nettle has tiny greenish flowers clustered along stalks that rise from the leaf axils.

While the stinging nettle causes skin irritation, another plant that is found along this trail is often used to cure it. This is the jewelweed or spotted touch-me-not, which in

112

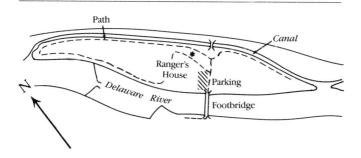

Path

Canal

Ranger's
House

Parking

N

Delaware River

Footbridge

summer bears pendant yellow flowers that have a curled
spur at the rear. These flowers are spotted with varying
amounts of red. If you crush the plant's succulent stem, a
juice is exuded; this juice can be spread on the skin to
relieve itching from poison ivy and insect bites.

If you take this walk in October, you may notice the
jewelweed for another reason. Its seeds mature in spring-
loaded pods which snap open when touched to eject and
distribute the seeds—thus its other common name. It is
almost impossible to walk this trail without brushing
against these seed pods, and after the first startling
encounter with them, one becomes accustomed to their
constant popping.

Continue along the canal, which in this section is
topped by trees arching toward the water. The predomi-
nant trees here are silver maple and river birch, both
commonly found in bottomland forests such as this. Silver
maple is identified by its six-inch, deeply cleft leaves
which have serrated margins. The underside of the foliage
is whitish gray, and often shows when the leaves are
blown by the wind.

River birch is more easily distinguished by its bark than
by its leaves. The shaggy bark varies from smooth reddish
brown flakes on the youngest branches to rough, almost
black, plates on the lower trunk. Its leaves are wedge
shaped, and more pointed than those of the more familiar
black, white, or yellow birches.

Delaware and Raritan Canal State Park 113

The river birch is important to a number of birds which breed on the island, supplying both nesting material and a site upon which to build the nest. Some of the birds of the bottomland forest prefer to nest near, or even over, the water, and the river birch often provides such a site. Its shreddy bark is a major constituent of the nests of some of these birds. This is true of the nests of the yellow-throated and cerulean warblers, and the blue-gray gnatcatcher, which also uses catkins from the river birch in building its nest.

All three of these birds are near the northern limit of their range here, and this makes Bull's Island a frequent stop for many birdwatchers. Another species near its northern limit, but which is more often seen than heard along here is the Acadian flycatcher, whose loud "peetsuh" call is sure to attract attention. The Acadian flycatcher has a great affinity for streams and brooks, and its nest usually hangs from a low branch out over the water.

You may have noticed how silty the soil is along the trail—a consequence of the nature of the floodplain and the floodplain forest. Floodplains are well-defined, flat valleys that are periodically flooded. When this flooding occurs, friction along the river's banks causes the rising waters to slow down and drop some of the sediment they are carrying. The largest sediments, sand and pebbles, are dropped closest to the banks, while the finer particles (silt) are carried to the outer reaches of the floodplain, where they are deposited. As a result, the area adjacent to the river is higher and better drained than the outer area, which tends to be waterlogged much of the time.

The footpath eventually gets wider and is paved with cobblestones; this is the remains of an old road, which ran parallel to the canal. Continue on this path until you reach a small cement aqueduct. When the Delaware is low, you can walk out onto the exposed shallow bank and look upriver. This bank is covered with loosestrife and willow, which can tolerate even more moisture than the plants of the floodplain behind. While surveying the river from here, you may spy a belted kingfisher scanning the water from an overhanging perch or plunging headlong to catch a fish. This handsome bird is blue gray above and white below. The male has a blue gray belt across the breast, and the female is similar but in addition has a chestnut band below. The kingfisher's large head, bushy crest, daggerlike bill, and raucous call further distinguish it.

The trail system is being extended, and if the water is low enough, you can cross the aqueduct and follow the new trail about $1/2$ mile south. Although plans exist to make a loop out of this trail, at present one must return the way one came.

Backtrack along the footpath, taking note of the many fallen trees along the way. With the abundant moisture available to these trees, most do not need deep taproots, and the periodic inundation the floodplain receives often knocks these shallow-rooted trees over. A variety of vines covers the fallen trees: poison ivy, Virginia creeper, bittersweet, and wild grape. Some of these trees are elms that have been killed by Dutch elm disease. Although we think of the elm as a widespread tree, this is because it is widely planted as an ornamental on lawns and along streets. In its natural setting, the American elm prefers the rich moist soil of the floodplain. A number of elms on this end of the island are still standing, though dead, and these snags provide a home for wildlife. The most beautiful resident of these gray hulks is the golden orange prothonotary warbler, which is unique among warblers in that it nests in tree cavities. Some ornithologists believe that this is an adaptation to habitats like floodplains, where cavities are numerous, but where dense bushes—the usual warbler nesting site—are scarce.

In spring, the spicebush's yellow flowers brighten the lower layer of this dark forest. Below the spicebush, two flowers of the arum family are common. Skunk cabbage, familiar to everyone, thrives in the wet soil of the floodplain.

Raven Rock, near Bull's Island

Its flower, which can be seen as early as February and March, is enclosed in a shell-like spathe, mottled and varying in color from green to purple brown. Inside, the strange-looking flowers are borne on a heavy, rounded stem called a spadix. Flies and other pollinators are attracted to the flower by the plant's strong odor.

The other common arum here is jack-in-the-pulpit, which is recognized by its pinnately compound leaf suggestive of poison ivy. Like the skunk cabbage's flower, the jack-in-the-pulpit's consists of a vertical spathe—the pulpit—wrapped around a spadix—Jack—which bears the flowers. In late summer the spathe withers, and a conical cluster of red berries is revealed.

After reaching the entrance road, cross it and bear right, going down onto the grassy path that follows the canal. In the 1800s, when the canal was operating, canal boats occasionally plied their way along here, headed south toward Trenton. This stretch of the canal was built principally to serve as a feeder to the main part of the canal, which began at Trenton and ran all the way to New Brunswick.

One of the main cargoes on these canal boats was Stockton formation sandstone, familiar to many as brownstone building stone. Many of the older homes in this area were built with brownstone (one can be seen just north of the park entrance on NJ 29), which also made its way into some well known buildings in cities along the canal. Old Queens at Rutgers in New Brunswick, and Nassau Hall at Princeton are two such historic buildings.

Along with the sandstone quarried at Lambertville, Stockton, and here at Raven Rock, this area provided another economically important rock—diabase traprock. Like the traprock of the Palisades, it is still quarried for use as road metal and concrete aggregate. In months when the foliage is not too dense, one of these traprock cliffs can be seen to the right beyond the canal and NJ 29. The village

Box elder, Bull's Island

of Raven Rock gets its name from this striking black rock outcrop.

Today, wood ducks and Canada geese replace the canal boats, and these and other waterfowl are commonly seen floating along the waters of the old canal. The primarily vegetarian ducks and geese feed on the foliage and seeds of a variety of aquatic plants which grow in and along the canal.

The path eventually comes out to a cleared area at the northern tip of the island. This spot offers a nice vantage of the Delaware River, and is a good place in spring and fall to see migrating geese, ducks, and hawks. Occasionally, an osprey will pause in its long journey to circle the river in search of fish in the waters below.

Follow the gravel path that leads along the river from this cleared area. You will see many sycamores on this part of the island, some of them quite large. The sycamore has distinctive mottled bark that flakes off in jigsawlike pieces, exposing the yellowish underbark. The three- to five-lobed toothed leaves and round, long-stalked fruits are equally distinctive. Although the sycamore is occasionally topped in height by the tulip tree, it is generally recognized as the most massive tree in the eastern United States. Many of the sycamores here are over 3 feet in diameter and over 100 feet tall. The Delaware Indians prized the sycamore for their dugout canoes.

The gravel road turns left at the end of the camping area and leads out to a paved road. Take this road to the right, back to the ranger station and entrance road. Turn right and follow the road past the parking lot to the footbridge over the Delaware. From the footbridge, there is a wonderful view of the river, and of the tall trees of Bull's Island's floodplain forest. Before returning to the car, it is worth crossing over to the Pennsylvania side of the river to the lovely town of Lumberville. If you turn right after crossing the footbridge and walk along the road a short distance, you reach the site of lock 12 of the Delaware Canal, which was operated by the state of Pennsylvania between 1831 and 1858.

16. Washington Crossing State Park

Distance: 2 ¹/₂ miles (Easy)
Walking time: 1¹/₄ hours
Directions: The park is located near the intersection of
Route 29 and Route 546 in Mercer County, eight miles
north of Trenton. The entrance is on 546, which should
not be confused with Route 579, where the park office is
located. Follow signs to the visitor's center, and park
there. The park is open during daylight hours throughout
the year. The visitor's center is open Wednesday through
Sunday 9 A.M. to 4:30 P.M., but hours may vary.
(609) 737-9304

In the fall of 1776, Gen. George Washington and the
soldiers of the Continental Army began a retreat from Fort
Lee to Pennsylvania. In skirmish after skirmish, the Continental Army had proved no match for the well-trained
British troops, and with Washington and his army trying to
regroup across the river, the British settled into winter
quarters at Trenton. It looked to many as if the colonies
would never break free of British rule.

Then, on Christmas night 1776, the Continental Army
crossed the icy waters of the Delaware River and the next
day marched to Trenton where, in a daring surprise attack,
they defeated the British, and, some historians believe,
turned the tide of the Revolutionary War. This walk takes
you past the spot where Washington and his army first
landed after crossing the Delaware, and along a portion of
the route the soldiers took to Trenton.

Before beginning your walk, you may wish to visit the
visitor's center, which has displays of colonial artifacts and
an audiovisual orientation to the park. From the visitor's
center, walk straight out past the flagpoles to meet
Continental Lane, the road over which the Continental

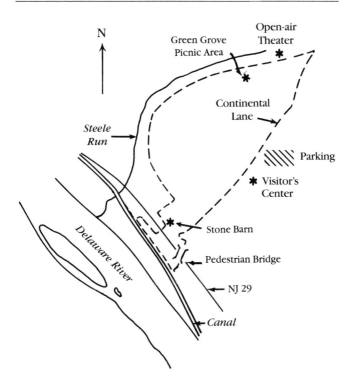

Army began its march to Trenton in 1776. Bear left onto this lane, which is flanked on either side by dogwood trees. The pink and white blossoms of the dogwood make this section of the walk particularly lovely in spring.

Follow this lane past the forest nursery on the left to where it ends near a large stone barn. This colonial structure served as the barn for the family living in the Ferry House, which is just across the road. In the barn are displays that depict the evolution of the United States flag from the flags of the earliest explorers to that of the present day, as well as a diorama of Washington and his men crossing the Delaware. The Ferry House, built around 1740, was a guest tavern and innkeeper's residence during

Washington Crossing State Park 121

the Revolution. Washington apparently took shelter from the storm here that Christmas night and worked out the plan of attack on the British stronghold at Trenton. From the Ferry House, walk up the hill and go right on the gravel path, which passes an overlook of the Delaware River.

The trail then leads to a pedestrian bridge; follow this bridge down to the river bank, where there is a reproduction of a wooden ferryboat like the ones used by the Continental Army in their famous river crossing, which took place at this point.

Backtrack to the pedestrian bridge, and walk underneath it to come out by a grassy path along a narrow waterway. This is the feeder of the Delaware and Raritan Canal, which runs south from Raven Rock (see Bull's Island Walk 15) to Trenton. The feeder was built in 1834 to keep the main canal full, as well as to transport cargo. By 1870, muskrat, who constantly dug holes in the banks, and the railroads, which hauled freight faster than canal boats, had joined to put the Delaware and Raritan Canal out of business.

Follow the canal for about $1/3$ mile until you reach a picnic area, then walk out to the road and turn right. Cross the road near the white gate and walk toward the stone barn. As you approach the barn, follow the road to the left, which leads into a plantation of red pines. The red pine grows naturally only in a small area in the very northern part of New Jersey, but you are likely to see it anywhere in the state, as it is planted widely for reforesting cut-over areas. The pines then grow into pure, even-aged stands like this one, which though pleasant to walk through, are biological deserts. Except for a few shade-tolerant ferns, mosses, and fungi, there is little plant life, and few animals make their home here.

Just as the road starts swinging left, turn left onto a grassy trail. You gradually pass out of the pine plantation into deciduous woods of red oak, red maple, and tulip

Christmas fern, Washington Crossing State Park

trees. The trail comes to a creek—Steele Run—flanked by large white oaks. These oaks are extremely important to the most common mammal found in such woods, the gray squirrel, who prefers white oak acorns to any other food. Although there are many white oaks in this forest, most are fairly young and do not bear a heavy crop of acorns; in fact, the first crop does not appear until the tree is about twenty years old. It would take the acorns of fifty twenty-year-old trees to sustain a single squirrel through the winter.

As you walk along the creek, note the outcrops of layered reddish rock to your left; this is Brunswick shale, so named because of its outcropping along the Raritan River at New Brunswick. Brunswick shale began as one of the sediments laid down in the area known as the Newark basin, which was formed about 190 million years ago. At that time, large blocks of the earth's crust were lifted and tilted to form mountains. Over time, thousands of feet of sediments were washed down from these mountains into the Newark basin and were deposited in broad, flat alluvial fans which later became rock. While these sediments were being laid down, dinosaurs and other long-extinct reptiles roamed the Newark basin, and coelacanths and six-foot-long amphibians swam in the Triassic swamps and ponds. Fossils of many of these ancient animals are turned up frequently, especially in the brownstone quarries scattered throughout the Newark basin.

The trail passes over a small footbridge, where the stream has again exposed the underlying bedrock. An understory of dogwood and a shrub layer of witch hazel and spicebush thrive on this gentle slope, and Christmas fern is conspicuous along the ground in some places. The largest of the evergreen ferns native to this area, Christmas fern is easily recognized by the shape of its pinnae (leaflets), which look like small green Christmas stockings. This is less likely the origin of the plant's name than the fact that it is one of the few ferns that is still green at Christmas.

The trail continues past a small beech grove and a few scattered elms which still appear healthy. In the 1930s, a fungus known as Dutch elm disease was introduced to this continent, and it spread rapidly, wiping out thousands of elms throughout the country. The disease is spread from tree to tree by a native bark beetle, which picks up the fungus when it bores its hole in the bark, then carries the fungal spores with it to the next tree.

The trail passes through the Green Grove picnic area. Beyond the picnic area, the stream is flanked by hemlocks and rhododendron, and for a minute, it feels as if you are walking along a ravine along the Kittatinny Ridge. Just after passing the open-air theater to your left, the trail crosses an asphalt road, follows the creek for another 75 yards, and then merges, at the top of a small hill, with Continental Lane. Turn right here and follow this trail $1/2$ mile to reach the Visitor Center parking lot.

17. Salem

Distance: 2 miles (Easy)
Walking time: 1^1/$_2$ hours
Directions: Take NJ 49 to Salem, where it becomes
Broadway. Park in the lot at the corner of Front St. and W.
Broadway, across the street from a large pale-blue building
with a sign identifying the Port of Salem.

When Quaker John Fenwick stepped ashore here in 1675
and founded the first permanent English settlement on the
Delaware River, he had biblical visions in mind. He named
the place Salem, a reference to *shalom*, the Hebrew word
for peace, and when persuading other English Quakers to
cross over and join their friends in this new-found para-
dise, he described it as a "terrestrial Canaan . . . where the
land floweth with milk and honey." While the peaceful-
ness of the town was disturbed dramatically during the
Revolutionary and Civil wars and was at other times, no
doubt, in part a matter of perspective, the entire region
has been known for hundreds of years as a rich and
extremely productive agricultural area, a "garden state"
indeed.

Walk along the well-worn brick sidewalks of West
Broadway toward the center of town and consider that
this street, which once would have been covered with
oyster shells, may have been the route of one of the
nation's first cattle drives. As George Washington planned
his strategy for the survival of his troops and the success of
the revolutionary cause during the winter of 1777–78 at
Valley Forge, he was aware of the "terrestrial Canaan"
lying across the Delaware in south Jersey. He thus sent
Gen. Anthony Wayne and several detachments of men on a
foraging expedition into this area. Wayne arrived in Salem
on 19 February 1778, and during the next day or two he

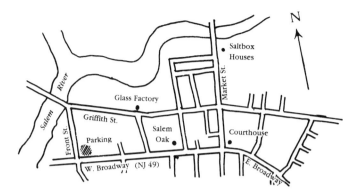

and his men succeeded in rounding up about 150 head of cattle from the surrounding countryside, in spite of the fact that some local farmers heard of the plan and hid their livestock in the swamps. After an unsuccessful attempt to ferry the cattle across the river to New Castle, Delaware, just a few miles from Salem, the soldiers drove the cattle along the river all the way to Trenton, crossed into Pennsylvania, and reached Valley Forge early in March, none too soon for the empty stomachs at the dispirited encampment.

The two-story rectangular red brick structure at 107 West Broadway, now occupied by a law firm, was originally the Orthodox Friends Meeting House. It was built in 1852, a replica of the Meeting House on East Broadway, to provide a separate place of worship for the Orthodox Quakers after they had broken from the Hicksite branch some twenty years earlier. The two main entrances facilitated another form of separation—between the men and the women assembling for worship.

Across the street is the Friends Burial Ground. Here the white, salt-block gravestones, many now diminished by the regular visitations of wind and rain, are shaded by a number of large and interesting trees, the grandest of which is the venerable Salem Oak. This virgin white oak

Salem Oak, Salem

has been part of the local landscape for over five hundred years, and John Fenwick reportedly sat beneath its branches in the autumn of 1675 when he bartered with the Lenape Indians for possession of the territory surrounding Salem.

Continue on Broadway to the Old Salem County Courthouse, a square, red brick building with a cannon in front, at the corner of Broadway and Market Street. For the first fifty or so years of the Salem settlement a small log cabin located near this spot served as the seat of government for Fenwick and his company of colonists. The present building has evolved from a structure erected on this site in 1735, but it is primarily the product of a thorough rebuilding undertaken in 1817 and of extensive remodeling done in 1908. During the latter work the entrance was moved from Market Street to its current location facing Broadway.

The steps of a courthouse have long been a prized platform for dramatic public demonstrations. Such was the case in September 1820 when, at least according to local legend, Col. Robert Gibbons Johnson, the wealthiest man in town and owner of numerous farms, ate a tomato on the steps of the courthouse here. At that time most farmers thought these "love apples," which Johnson had grown on his imported South American plants, were worthless and perhaps poisonous. The colonel apparently hoped that his saucy showmanship would encourage his contemporaries to catch up with his progressive plans to cultivate the tomato as a cash crop. The idea did, of course, catch on, and Salem County reaped some rich financial rewards as a result. Johnson was also instrumental in organizing local agricultural exhibitions and became one of the earliest historians of the city and county of Salem.

Another agricultural product for which Salem became quite well known during the second half of the nineteenth century was produced just down the street, in a frame building at the rear of 192 and 194 East Broadway. Here the milk that was by that time flowing freely in this terrestrial Canaan was transformed into the celebrated Salem ice cream. At his factory on East Broadway, John Bruna, whose original plant was established in 1852, could manufacture three thousand quarts of ice cream per day. Though Bruna initially intended to satisfy only local demands, the quality of his product became more widely known, and he began filling requests from throughout the state, as well as from Philadelphia and Washington, D.C.

The large volume of ice cream produced is perhaps in some way proportionate to the immensity of some of the livestock raised here. Many area farmers experimented with various methods of fattening cattle, but the art of feeding was evidently perfected by one Job Tyler. In 1823 a special steamer came to Salem from Philadelphia to transport one of Tyler's oxen to market. This ox, after being slaughtered and dressed, tipped the scales at 2,652 pounds. But such bovine bravado was not the only source of pride for Salem County livestock growers; many also raised whole herds of hogs averaging over 500 pounds each, with some reaching more than twice that weight.

These indications of agricultural abundance are even more significant when one realizes that they emerged from an area that only a few decades earlier was on the verge of becoming an agricultural wasteland. A century of intense farming had stripped the soil of its nutrients, and around the turn of the nineteenth century it became unable to sustain the farmers' crops. Many Salemites began leaving the area, moving west into Pennsylvania, the Midwest, the Great Plains, and even to the West Coast. Apparently unconcerned about the possible confusion or competition it might eventually engender, members of the Street family founded new Salems as they migrated westward—Salem, Ohio, in 1803; Salem, Indiana, in 1815; Salem, Iowa, in the 1820s; and Salem, Oregon, in 1844.

The region's agricultural future was revitalized, however, when a natural fertilizer called marl, common in New Jersey's Inner Coastal Plain, was discovered about 1810 and began to be distributed throughout the county. The results were dramatic. It was once again possible to grow wheat on the worn-out land, yields of corn increased from about fifteen to fifty bushels per acre, and cattle began grazing on fields set permanently apart for that purpose. New crops were also introduced, such as the Irish or round potato. It was found that fields fertilized with marl produced potatoes of a more uniformly smooth and attractive appearance than did fields treated with barnyard manure alone. The price of the product then shot up just like the plants, going from around twenty cents to over sixty cents per bushel. The rather aggressive agriculturists of Salem County were thus quite lucky that after pushing their production beyond the natural limits of the land, so effective a remedy was so easily found.

A little farther down on East Broadway, just past the site of the old ice cream factory, is the Salem Friends Meeting House. Built in 1772, this brick structure with walls eighteen inches thick was used as a temporary shelter by

British troops in 1778 and, after the war, served as an overflow courtroom for Tory trials. The date of construction is displayed in the patterned brickwork on the west end, a style developed by the Flemish-Norman artisans of France and found on a number of other buildings in Salem County.

Go back and turn right on Market Street; as you follow the sidewalk down Market past the old courthouse, you enter the most attractive section of the restored historic district. In the grassy lot beside the new courthouse is the Robert Johnson house, just a tomato's throw from the old courthouse steps. The imposing structure of the First Presbyterian Church was completed in 1856. The tall white steeple not only lifts one's eyes heavenward but, being lighted at night, has also guided many nocturnal travelers to the proffered peace of Salem. Across the street, at numbers 79–83, is the Alexander Grant House, which is now the home of the Salem County Historical Society. The House was built in the 1720s and contains the society's research library and a twenty-room museum furnished with antiques, Indian relics, and many other items that embody the heritage of the county.

At the end of the next block (16–18 Market Street) are two small saltbox houses. The wood frame structures (a third was destroyed by fire) date to about 1825 and are typical of many such houses found throughout the city. A central fireplace and chimney divides each house into what was originally two dwelling spaces, each with four rooms and an attic. Construction techniques included beaded paneling, mortise-and-tenon joinery, and hand-made hardware.

Across the street from the saltbox houses is a rustic little log cabin with an earthen roof. This reconstructed homestead, enframed by a wooden fence and with a door conducive to headaches, is called "New Sweden" and commemorates Salem's earliest European settlers. Swedes and Finns had come to the area about 1640, several decades before John Fenwick came to stay, and they did indeed have their share of headaches, not the least of which were the swarming hordes of mosquitoes. Fort Elfsborg, the military capital of the territory of New Sweden built in 1643 and located somewhere near present day Point Elsinboro, came to be called Fort Mosehettoesburg because of the insects that perhaps became the unwitting allies of the Dutch in their successful attempts to effect the exodus of the Swedes, and thus to gain control of the Delaware Valley fur trade. The Swedes resettled in the vicinity of today's Wilmington, Delaware.

Walk back along Market Street and turn right on Griffith Street, which is just past the Clement J. Acton House and St. John's Episcopal Church. Follow Griffith to an industrial area marked by blue buildings with an enclosed walkway crossing over the street. Continue under the suspended walkway down to the next corner where this manufacturing complex is identified as Plant 6 of the Anchor Glass Container Corporation.

Glassmaking became established early in Salem County, due in part to the quality of the local sand. The county can, in fact, take credit for the first glass produced in North America, an event that took place in 1739 at Caspar Wistar's glassworks about five miles from Salem. The plant here has its roots in the Salem Glass Works, which was established by Henry Hall, Joseph Pancoast, and John Craven in 1863 and which, within a decade, had become one of the world's largest manufacturers of hollow glassware. It was acquired by Anchor-Hocking in 1937.

Turn left on Fourth Street, just before the company's red brick headquarters, and you will see on your left a more recent concern of glassware companies—recycling. Here the different types and colors of glass resulting from the recycling efforts of local individuals and communities are sorted out, cleaned up, and ground down before being melted and mixed with various other materials to form the next generation of glass containers. The mounds of finely ground glass sparkling in the sunlight are a reminder that this process, aside from decreasing the amount of waste, reduces the need for sand and thus lessens the burden on the land, an idea of both historical and current significance in the well-worn lands of Salem County.

Take Fourth Street to Broadway, turn right, and follow it back to the parking lot by the dock.

18. Bridgeton

Distance: 2^1/$_2$ miles (Easy)
Walking time: 2 hours
Directions: Take NJ 77 (from the north) or NJ 49 (from the east or west) into Bridgeton and follow the signs to the New Jersey Tourist Information Center, which is located at the intersection of these two roads. The Center is open year round from 8:30 A.M. to 4:30 P.M. Monday through Friday, and during the summer is also open weekends and holidays from 10 A.M. to 4 P.M. (609) 451-4802.

When surveyor Richard Hancock decided in 1686 to build a sawmill and several worker's houses along a stretch of what is now called Mill Creek, just upstream from the Cohansey River in Cumberland County, he established the settlement that eventually grew into the city of Bridgeton. Thirty years later, in 1716, a bridge was constructed over the river and the community became known as Cohansey Bridge. In 1749 it was designated the county seat, though it contained only about fifteen buildings. The name of the settlement was Bridge Town from about 1765 to 1816, at which time the local bank printed the name incorrectly on its stationery, and it was apparently easier or more desirable to change the name of the town to "Bridge ton" than to reprint the stationery. In the three centuries since the building of Hancock's mill, Bridgeton has seen a variety of industrial endeavors come and go, including glass factories, canneries, and nail manufacturing, and has witnessed several notable historic events. Today it is the home of New Jersey's largest historic district.

From the Tourist Information Center, cross Broad Street (NJ 49) and head up Pearl Street (NJ 77 North). After one block turn right on McCormick Place (Warren Street), go

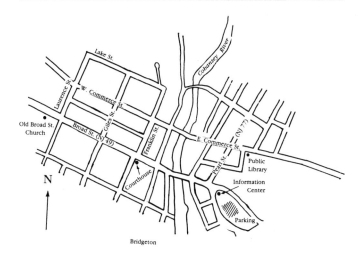

Bridgeton

one block and turn left on Orange Street. Notice on your right the Bridgeton Fire Department. This Victorian structure, built in 1898 of brick and covered with white stucco, is one of the oldest working firehouses in southern New Jersey. It originally housed horse-drawn equipment, the last piece of which was retired in 1920, and an authentic 1877 Silsby Steam Fire Engine is still on display. Also of interest are the drying tower for hoses and the brass sliding pole.

Just ahead, on the corner of Orange and Commerce streets, is the Bridgeton Free Public Library. The left-hand section of this building was formerly the Cumberland National Bank, which, when it was founded here in 1816, was the first bank in the state south of Camden and was the one whose misprinted letterhead resulted in Bridge Town becoming Bridgeton. It moved down the street in 1886, at which time the library moved in. The "free" in the library's name was meant to distinguish it from those that charged for their services and was a democratizing innovation that was a corollary of the campaign for tax-supported

Bridgeton Fire Department, Bridgeton

public education that began in the middle of the nineteenth century. This movement also led to the closing of three well-known private schools in Bridgeton—Ivy Hall Seminary, South Jersey Institute, and West Jersey Academy—around the turn of the century. On the lower level of the library is the George Woodruff Indian Museum, which houses an extensive collection of artifacts from the area's earliest inhabitants, the Leni-Lenape Indians.

Follow Commerce Street across Bank Street and past the Bridgeton City Hall and City Hall Annex (across the street); the latter was built in 1908 as a federal building for customs and a post office. At 186 East Commerce is St. Andrew's Episcopal Church. The Episcopalian influence in this area has been felt since the late seventeenth century, but regular services did not begin in Bridgeton until 1851, when they were conducted by priests from Salem. The present structure was consecrated on St. Andrew's Day in

1864. The bell in the belfry dates to 1867, and the pipe organ in the sanctuary to 1878.

After passing the church, turn left onto Walnut Street and notice the white two-story house with green shutters at 205 East Commerce. This house was built in 1850 and the bases and capitals of the columns on the porch were hand-carved by its owner. Take Walnut one block and then turn left on Cedar Street, following it down to Bank Street. Pause at this corner to observe a few architectural points of interest. First there is the eclectic Victorian house with twin towers at 62–64 Bank that was built in 1900 by Reuben Hunt and his brother R. Winfield Hunt. Then, at number 60, is a brown house with green shutters; it sports two ironwork porches that were done in 1840 by the blacksmith who built the house. The large, squarish building on your left is Brearley Lodge, constructed in 1797 as both a Masonic hall and a home for the Harmony School. The Lodge's foundation is made of local sandstone; the mansard roof was added about 1870.

Take Bank Street past the lodge, back down to Commerce Street, and turn right. Follow Commerce through the downtown area, with its numerous Victorian buildings and shops, and across the river to Atlantic Street. This street forms the entrance to Bridgeton City Park, which in its 1,200 acres contains, among other attractions, a lake, a 1$^{1}/_{2}$-mile-long millrace dug by hand in 1814, a large zoo, and the Nanticoke Lenape Village, reconstructed to depict Indian life in the seventeenth century. Just within the park entrance on the right is a one-story cream-colored building that from 1815 to the 1890s was the office of the Cumberland Nail and Iron Company. One of the machines used in the nail-production process is on display in back of the building.

Continue on Commerce Street for one block and turn right on Franklin Street, following it into a section of stately homes and turning left on Lake Street. At 25 Lake is the 1872 structure known locally as the House of Seven

Old Broad Street Church, Bridgeton

Gables. This house, which has served at times as a private school and as a maternity hospital, incorporates the Gothic Revival designs of architect James Simms, whose work can also be seen in similar structures in Philadelphia. Turn left on Giles Street and then right one block later on Commerce. At the next intersection, turn left on Lawrence Street and take it down to Broad Street. On the opposite corner you will see what is perhaps the most enduring and attractive historic structure in Bridgeton—the Old Broad Street Church.

The two acres of land containing the church and cemetery were donated in 1791 by a Quaker named Mark Miller for the purpose of building a public place of worship for the Bridgeton community, which then consisted of about three hundred people. Construction began in July 1792 with the bricks being made my hand at the site and with the main door facing Broad Street, before this road was rerouted to its present location on the opposite side of the church. When the structure was about halfway finished, funds ran out and a lottery, authorized by the legislature, was instituted in order to raise an additional two thousand dollars. The dedication service was held in May of 1795, the year the church shed its independent status and became officially associated with the Presbyterian church.

The interior of this well-preserved Georgian structure features a pulpit shaped like a wine glass, brick-paved aisles, original whale-oil lamps, and two cast-iron stoves that date to about 1810. Sunday services are still held here during the summer. The cemetery holds the tree-shaded graves of many colonial patriots, whose names appear on a memorial stone inscribed with a phrase from the Declaration of Independence.

From the church, take Broad Street back toward the center of town for one block and turn left on Giles Street. At the corner of Giles and Commerce you will see the red doors of the newer home of the first Presbyterian Church. Turn right here and walk along West Commerce, which reflects the prosperity enjoyed by many Bridgetonians during the second half of the nineteenth century as they reaped the financial fruits of the growing city's various industries. Both Greek revival and Victorian influences are evident in many of these houses. Note especially the Nixon house at number 81, which was constructed in 1851, just a few years before its architect, Thomas U. Walter, began designing the dome for the U.S. Capitol building, and at number 65, the eyebrow windows and widow's walk atop the Elmer house, built around 1834.

Turn right on Franklin Street and follow it back to Broad. The large building facing you at this intersection is the Cumberland County Courthouse. This structure is the last of a succession of four courthouses built in this vicinity, the earlier ones having been either destroyed by fire or razed to make way for the next. On display in the main corridor of the courthouse is one of the city's most prized possessions—the Bridgeton Liberty Bell. The bell was purchased by the citizens in 1765 to hang in the courthouse cupola. On 7 July 1776 it summoned these citizens to the courthouse steps for a reading of the freshly signed Declaration of Independence. Local residents are fond of saying that the only difference between their Liberty Bell and the more famous one in Philadelphia is that theirs isn't cracked.

Take Broad Street toward the river and notice the square wooden building with a stone base across from the courthouse. This is Potter's Tavern, which was built in the late 1760s and soon became a popular community meeting place. During the 1770s many of the conversations here naturally centered on the issue of American independence, and a number of the revolutionaries finally decided to express their views in writing. Their handwritten bulletins, called the *Plain Dealer,* were first posted here at the tavern on Christmas Day 1775 and appeared again each Thursday morning for a couple of months. The *Plain Dealer* was thus New Jersey's first, though short-lived, newspaper, and helped to heighten the revolutionary fervor among the citizens of Bridgeton. Two of the paper's authors, Ebenezer Elmer and Joseph Bloomfield, later became governors of New Jersey. Another, Dr. Jonathan Elmer, was the first U.S. senator elected from New Jersey and was the man who read the Declaration of Independence from the courthouse steps across the street.

Just down the hill from the tavern, at the corner of Broad and Atlantic, is a stone structure built in 1799 by George Burgin, an early sheriff of Bridgeton. This building served as a warehouse for goods arriving by ship. During much of the city's history, the Cohansey River has been a busy commercial waterway, with thirty cargo ships based here in the mid-nineteenth century. Steamboats also plied these waters, especially after 1845, when regular service began between Bridgeton and Philadelphia. In the early 1860s the steamboats encountered some fierce new competition as the West Jersey Railroad began providing a more direct route to the metropolis. Continuing with your more pedestrian mode of transportation, follow Broad Street across the river and back to the Tourist Information Center, which is just ahead on your right.

The Inner Coastal Plain

Cattail marsh, near Cranbury
Courtesy Robichaud and Buell

19. Cheesequake State Park

Distance: 3^1/$_2$ miles (Moderate)
Walking time: 2 hours
Directions: Take the Garden State Parkway to exit 120 and
turn right onto Matawan Rd. Go ^{1}/$_2$ mile and turn right
onto Cliffwood Ave. Turn right on Gordon Ave. and go ^{7}/$_{10}$
mile to the park entrance. Continue past the entrance ^{1}/$_8$
mile to the parking area on the left. From Memorial Day
weekend to Labor Day there is a parking fee of $5.00 on
weekdays and $7.00 on weekends and holidays. Tuesdays
are free. (908) 566–2161

Close to the sprawling metropolis of northeastern New
Jersey, Cheesequake State Park preserves an extensive salt
marsh, a small cedar swamp, and an interesting variety of
plant and animal life. Because of its proximity to this
metropolis and also to the mosquito-harboring salt
marshes, it is best to visit the park in late fall or early
spring, when the summertime crowds of visitors and
biting insects can be avoided.

Follow the yellow-green-red-blazed trail which leads
away from the parking lot through woods of white oak,
sassafras, and black gum trees. To the left, a small brook
follows the trail as it flows toward Cheesequake Creek.
Flanked by sweet pepperbush, this shallow brook is
reminiscent of the cripples that meander along the level
sand of the Pine Barrens to the south.

The trail (now with a red-green blaze) swings left over a
small footbridge and leads past a moist hollow which is
filled with ferns. Christmas fern, cinnamon fern, and
spinulose woodfern are among the ferns that thrive in the
protection of this gradual north-facing slope. The trail then
reaches a knoll that is obviously drier than the area
traversed so far: chestnut oaks and scattered pitch pines

144

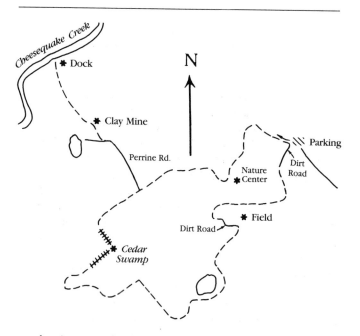

predominate on this knoll, with a layer of drought-tolerant shrubs such as huckleberry and blueberry below. The Nature Center is located at the top of this hill (open Wednesday through Sunday 10 A.M. to 3 P.M.).

The trail passes over a series of small creeks, each one flanked by moisture-loving shrubs and trees, and then climbs up a series of steps to reach another dry knoll. The trail intersects with a sandy trail, on which you should bear right, and a short distance further it reaches Perrine Road; turn right again and follow this sand road about 1/4 mile to an open area.

This area was formerly mined for clay, as is suggested by the spoil banks that can be seen scattered about. The clay here as well as that underlying Cheesequake marsh was deposited during the Cretaceous period, at a time when the sea was encroaching upon the New Jersey coastal plain. Nearby rivers then deposited their sediments into the estuaries of this advancing sea. Unlike older sedimentary deposits in New Jersey, these sediments have remained unconsolidated; that is, they have not become rock.

The clay beds here were worked principally for pottery clay during the years when New Jersey's ceramic industry, centered at Trenton, still used native clay deposits. Today, clays from outside New Jersey are used, though clay beds are still worked in nearby South Amboy and Sayreville to provide the raw material for bricks and terra cotta.

There is a good view of the marsh from here, and also of Perrine's Pond, which is off to the left. In fall, this vista is often filled with migrating hawks. Kestrels perch on the snag next to the pond, while sharp-shinned hawks chase each other over the marsh. Ospreys on their way south can occasionally be seen circling overhead, as they pause momentarily to hunt the waters of Cheesequake Creek.

One raptor which can be seen here year round is the northern harrier, or marsh hawk, which continuously skims low over the marsh in search of rodents, reptiles, and small birds. The male marsh hawk is solid gray, while the female is brownish with dark streaking below. Both sexes have a conspicuous white rump patch. The marsh hawk's most distinctive feature is its flattened facial feathers. Like the facial disc of an owl, these feathers aid the marsh hawk in locating its prey by reflecting sound toward the ears.

Follow the road to the left and then immediately bear right on a path out to Cheesequake Creek. This path leads first through tall phragmites and then out over the marsh. Closest to the brackish waters of Cheesequake Creek grows salt-marsh cordgrass, or thatch grass, with its tough, round stems and long, coarse, sharply pointed leaves. Behind it, on parts of the marsh that are only reached by high tides, the slender, delicate salt-meadow grass predominates. Farmers used to harvest this grass as salt hay for their livestock.

146 *Cheesequake State Park*

Here and there on the marsh can be seen shallow depressions where very different plants are growing. These depressions, called pannes, are washed by the tides infrequently and remain dry for extended periods, during which the salt water evaporates. The salt left behind creates a very saline site, and only certain specialized plants can survive under these conditions. Two or three species of glasswort or samphire are most common, all of which are identified by their succulent, jointed stems and scalelike leaves. The glassworts add a touch of color in the fall, when they turn bright red.

Another plant that is commonly found in these saline depressions is orache, identified by its mealy, gray green, trowel-shaped leaves. Orache closely resembles lambsquarters or pigweed, the weed that is so familiar to many gardeners. The two plants are both members of the goosefoot family, as are the glassworts.

The trail ends near the bleached pilings of an old dock on Cheesequake Creek. In the late 1800s, local farmers brought fruits and vegetables to these docks to be picked up by steamboats, which carried the produce to the Amboys. Nowadays, the creek supports quieter traffic: in winter, canvasback, bufflehead, and ruddy ducks float along the lower end of the creek, while in summer, great egrets, snowy egrets, and green and great blue herons stalk the banks for crabs and fish.

Another animal of the salt marsh seen occasionally is the northern diamondback terrapin, a beautiful turtle identified by its boldly patterned sculpted carapace. Each of the large scutes (scales) of the carapace has distinctive concentric grooves and ridges. The terrapin feeds on fish, crabs, and other animals which it finds in the creek. Severely reduced in number by market hunting in the late 1800s and early 1900s, the terrapin is today making a comeback.

Backtrack to the sand road, and then follow it back to the trail intersection. Turn right onto Cedar Trail, which has a green blaze. The trail soon ascends a low knoll overlooking the marsh before descending to a boardwalk which crosses a swampy area. Jewelweed, sweet pepperbush, tearthumb, and dodder form dense thickets here, providing ample cover for towhees, redwing blackbirds, phoebes, and other birds. The boardwalk envelops a red maple tree in the middle of the swamp; although it adapts to a wide variety of soil and moisture conditions, the red maple is most commonly found in damp areas like this one. Red maple is readily identified by its three-lobed, coarsely toothed leaves, its reddish, oppositely arranged twigs and buds, and by its samaras (seed cases), which are shaped like bees' wings. In early spring, sometimes while the snow is still on the ground, the red maple takes on a crimson cast from the blooming of its short clusters of small red flowers.

Beyond the boardwalk, the trail leads up a hill and then bears right before reaching another boardwalk, this one leading through an Atlantic white cedar swamp. On even the hottest summer days, these dense cedars create a cool microclimate which provides welcome relief from the blazing sun.

At the end of the boardwalk, follow the trail out to Museum Road and turn left. Follow this road about $1/3$ mile to where it intersects the green-blazed trail (just past a small, open, partially blacktopped area on the right). Turn right here and immediately bear left at the fork. The trail skirts the edge of a marsh and then passes through woods of black birch, red maple, and red and white oak. The forest floor here is carpeted with Canada mayflower, whose small white flowers dot the ground in May. Like many of the herbs of the oak forest, Canada mayflower spreads by means of underground runners.

As the trail nears a small stream, it encounters a narrow swath of bottomland trees. The huge tulip and sycamore trees here are humbling in their proportions. The trail crosses a small section of boardwalk flanked by Japanese knotweed, then enters more oak woods. After skirting the edge of a small pond, largely overgrown with vegetation, the trail winds past scattered beech and sweet gum trees before reaching another dirt road. Turn left here and follow the road past the picnic area and field, then turn right onto the green trail again.

About $1/3$ mile further, the trail reaches a dirt road. Turn right here and follow this road back to the parking area.

20. Burlington

Distance: 1³/₄ miles (Easy)
Walking time: 1¹/₂ hours
Directions: Take US 130 to Burlington and exit on County
Rd. 541 North (High St., opposite 541 South). Follow
High St. through town and park in the large parking lot by
the Delaware River, across from the Hope Steam Fire
Engine Company.

The historic city of Burlington has been shaped over the
past three centuries largely by the triple influences of the
Quakers, the Episcopalians, and the Delaware River. When
two companies of Quakers founded the city in 1677, they
designed it so that the group from Yorkshire would live on
the east side of High Street, while those from London
would live on the west. The Colonial Assembly established
Burlington as the capital of the Province of West New
Jersey in 1681, and a variety of industries, including a
pottery, a sawmill, and a shipyard, as well as various
educational endeavors, began to develop. The Episcopalians arrived in 1702 and began their own religious and
educational institutions, often, it seems, with some
antagonism toward the Quakers. The river, of course, has
always been here.

   From the parking lot, cross over to the right-hand side of
High Street, which is lined with buildings of historical
interest. On the corner, at number 202, is the John
Hoskins House, built in 1797. This building has served as a
model for other restoration work in the city and is cur-
rently the home of the City of Burlington Historical
Society. A little further on, near the curb just before
Temple Bnai Israel, is a historic marker indicating the
place where once stood the office of Samuel Jennings, a
Quaker minister who was deputy governor from 1681 to

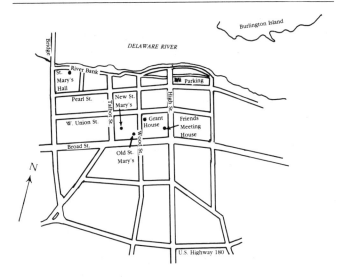

1684. In this office, around 1730, Benjamin Franklin
established what was apparently the first copperplate
printing operation in America. He printed a variety of
government documents and birth certificates, as well as
the first currency for the province. Several decades later,
Isaac Collins, former "Printer to the King," presided over
the shop and produced New Jersey's first long-running
weekly newspaper, the *New Jersey Gazette,* consisting of
a single nine-by-fourteen-inch folio sheet. This paper,
inspired by the Revolution and dedicated to supporting
the "Interests of Religion and Liberty," first appeared on
5 December 1777 and continued until 1786.

At 301 High Street is the Burlington Pharmacy
(Wheatley's), which is the oldest continuous pharmacy in
the state. Isaac Collins rented rooms here during the
1770s, and from its steps John Greenleaf Whittier, Quaker
poet and political activist, preached a nineteenth-century
plea for the abolition of slavery.

Further down along the right-hand side of the street,
behind the brick wall and iron gate, is the Friends Meeting

House. Quakers have gathered at this site for worship and silent communion for over three hundred years, originally in a hexagonal structure built in 1685, and then in the present building constructed in 1785. Here modern-day members of the Society of Friends still use eighteenth-century seats and tables amid a typically austere interior, the unadorned style of which can be seen through the large windows along the left-hand side of the building. Immediately in back of the Meeting House is an enormous sycamore tree, beside which is a small memorial to Indian Chief Ockanickon, who was buried here in 1681. The plaque on the rock records his final words: "Be plain and fair to all, both Indian and Christian as I have been."

Continue on the path leading through the cemetery, the oldest in Burlington, noting the simplicity of the Quaker gravestones, which date from as early as 1744. Exit through the gate at the rear and go left to West Broad Street. Arriving at the corner of Wood and West Broad streets, you can see a small, one-story brick building to your left. This is the Surveyor General's Office, also known as the Proprietors' Office. Among the many historic documents housed here is the original Concessions and Agreements of West Jersey, a statement of governmental principles such as trial by jury, the secret ballot, and absolute religious toleration, devised largely by William Penn and adopted in 1677.

Running down the middle of West Broad is another distinctive feature of Burlington. These railroad tracks have carried trains and caused commotion among the citizens from 1834 until the present. The city council ordered the tracks removed in 1926, a resolution which resulted only in some minor modifications regarding warning whistles and speed limits.

The small stucco building on the corner of Wood and West Broad is Old St. Mary's Church, which was the first Episcopal building in New Jersey and housed the first American parish of the Church of England's missionary

Memorial to Chief Ockanickon, Burlington

Society for the Propagation of the Gospel. This structure, built in 1703, shows the architectural influence of the Church of England in its early Georgian Colonial design. During the American Revolution, the Loyalist cause was propounded from this pulpit as the preachers attempted to persuade the colonists of George III's sovereignty.

Walk along West Broad past Old St. Mary's, noting the cemetery, where many prominent figures from Burlington's past—such as Elias Boudinot, president of the Continental Congress—are buried. It was originally called the Christian burying ground to distinguish it from the Quaker burying ground, though, today at least, the difference in the style of tombstones is more than sufficient to set them apart. Go through the archway into the churchyard of New St. Mary's. The walkway here has been designated the Bishop's Walk in memory of three bishops of New Jersey who have been associated with this church, foremost among them George Washington Doane, who was the second Bishop of New Jersey and the eighth rector of the Burlington parish.

The impressive building before you was designed by Richard Upjohn, the architect of Trinity Church in New York City and many other historic buildings displaying the Gothic Revival style. Completed in 1854 under the supervision of Bishop Doane, this National Historic Landmark is one of the earliest cruciform buildings in the United States. Enter the church through the small door on the left. The pleasing interior design reflects the form and feeling of the original church, with many stained-glass windows and wooden furnishings, but it is actually of rather recent vintage; a fire in 1976 severely damaged most of the interior, and the restoration work was completed in 1986.

Exit the churchyard through the gate on the right and continue along West Broad Street to Talbot Street. Turn right on Talbot and follow it alongside the cemetery down to West Union Street, where you will take another right. One block ahead is Wood Street, where the many attractive and historic homes give the area a distinctly eighteenth-century flavor. To the right, set back from the street at number 309, is the Ulysses S. Grant House. Grant's family lived in this two-story stucco dwelling with French windows and wrought-iron railings in 1864 and 1865 while the general was leading the Union Army in the Civil War. He visited occasionally and was en route here when he received news of Lincoln's assassination; he returned immediately to Washington.

Follow Wood Street to the north, back across West Union, through the section that has been dubbed Professor's Row because many teachers from St. Mary's Hall and the Burlington Academy have lived here. Just past number 217 is the Revell House. This small brick house, built in 1685 by a wealthy Quaker distiller named George Hutchinson, is the oldest building in the county and, perhaps, in the state. Thomas Revell, who was the first clerk of the Burlington Court and also served on the West Jersey Council, used the house as an office during the 1690s. Benjamin Franklin, after missing his ferry back to

New St. Mary's Church, Burlington

Philadelphia one day, apparently received a piece of gingerbread from a generous woman in this house. To commemorate this event, or at least to celebrate the legend, gingerbread is sold at the Wood Street Fair, held annually on the first Saturday after Labor Day, with proceeds going for the upkeep of the Revell, or Ginger-bread, House.

Go left at the next corner onto West Pearl Street. Follow Pearl for one block and then turn right on Talbot, leading toward the river. Go left on Riverbank and take it down to St. Mary's Hall-Doane Academy, which is just this side of the Burlington-Bristol Bridge. This private Episcopal school, attended for a time by General Grant's daughter, was founded in 1837 by Bishop Doane. When the Reverend Henry Caswall, a Church of England clergyman, came to Burlington to visit the bishop in 1854, he recorded his impressions of this site as follows:

> The situation of Burlington College, the episcopal residence, and St. Mary's Hall, is truly delightful. The grounds extend over forty acres, on the bank of the

Delaware, which is at this point a magnificent stream, like the Ohio or the Mississippi. Vessels were passing in constant succession, including brigs of 400 or 500 tons. The grounds were laid out in the English style by the bishop himself, whose own hands planted most of the trees which now overshadow the pleasant walks. The buildings are supplied with the pure water of the river by a hydraulic apparatus, and lighted with their own gas, which is manufactured on the spot.*

Obviously, things have changed somewhat during the subsequent century and a half. But the waters of the Delaware, though no longer so pure, continue to roll by, carrying ships that in the past would have stopped here to other ports such as Camden, Philadelphia, and Trenton. Burlington was indeed a thriving maritime center for many years, having been designated in 1681 as the principal port of entry for West Jersey; during the mid-eighteenth century it rivaled the ports of Philadelphia, New York, and Boston. This fact contributed to the area's industrial and commercial development, which led in turn to the addition of other immigrants and ethnic groups to the population.

Follow Riverbank back the way you came, crossing over to the path along the river if you like, and on the right-hand side of the road just after the point where the path becomes a paved sidewalk, you will find a small memorial to the very first ship to come to Burlington. The tablet on the boulder inside the wrought-iron fence commemorates the arrival of the ship *Shield,* and with it a third company of Quakers, on 10 December 1678. During the following century, Burlington, being conveniently located on the main waterway between New York and Philadelphia, became a popular summer resort area for wealthy urban-ites. The several substantial estates here along the river are

* From Miriam V. Studley, *Historic New Jersey Through Visitors' Eyes* (Princeton, N.J.: Van Nostrand, 1964), 139–140.

Revell House, Burlington

evidence of this influence and, of course, are ideally located to afford a nice view of the river and, on hot summer days, to benefit from its breezes.

Continue along the riverside walk and pause at the flagpoles. Beyond them lies Burlington Island, which was settled by Europeans more than fifty years before the Quakers came to Burlington City. In 1624 the ship *New Netherland,* owned by the Dutch West India Company, arrived here at what was originally called Matinicunk Island, with several families and single men on board. They built a fort and trading post to barter with the Native Americans and constructed bark huts patterned after the native dwellings, thus establishing the first European settlement in New Jersey. These original settlers were removed to Manhattan Island in 1626 and for the following fifty years control of Burlington Island shifted back and forth between Dutch, Swedish, and English hands. Legal action initiated in 1682 and finalized in 1710 gave owner-ship of the island to the city of Burlington, with the proposal that revenue from the rental of farm land and the sale of timber from the island be used to support the city's schools. In the early twentieth century, thousands of visitors flocked daily during the summer to a family picnic resort on the downstream end of the island. This resort evolved into a very popular and successful amusement park with a variety of rides, including a giant roller coaster. Most of the park was destroyed by fire in 1928.

From the flagpoles, an area that was formerly a public wharf and a point from which passengers have crossed the river since 1680, the parking lot is just down the sidewalk and across the street.

21. Rancocas State Park

Distance: 2^1/2 miles (Easy)

Walking time: 1^1/2 hours

Directions: From Interstate 295, take exit 45A and go right on Rancocas Rd. about 1^3/4 miles to the Rancocas Nature Center entrance (on the right). Park in the lot just beyond the center. The park and center are open 9:00 A.M. to 5:00 P.M. daily except Mondays and holidays. Dogs are not allowed on the trail. (609) 261-2495

Rancocas State Park, an 1,100-acre area along the north and south branches of Rancocas Creek, is located in the physiographic region known as the Inner Coastal Plain. The Inner Coastal Plain serves as the transportation corridor for traffic between the northeast's major cities, and as such, has undergone extensive industrial, commercial, and residential development. Those areas that are not devoted to these uses have been cleared for fruit, vegetable, dairy, and poultry farming. As a result, little forested area remains in this region. Rancocas State Park, in addition to preserving extensive lowland areas, preserves an interesting array of upland forest types.

Before you begin your walk, stop at the Rancocas Nature Center, which is operated by the New Jersey Audubon Society. The center contains a small museum area, a book and gift shop, and a reference library.

From the parking lot, walk to the field beyond the barn and the shed at the end of the driveway. Two mowed trails run out into this field; take the left one. A variety of plants typical of abandoned fields grows along this trail. A surprising number of these plants are not native to this continent, but were brought here from Europe by early settlers. Some plants were introduced accidentally, but many were brought knowingly as garden herbs.

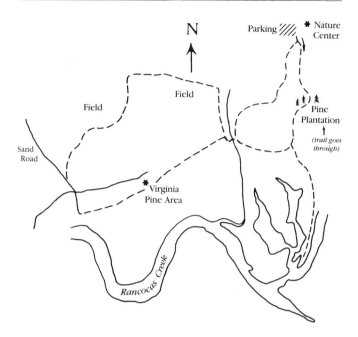

One such plant that is common in this field is Queen
Anne's lace, also known as wild carrot, since it is a close
relative of our domestic carrot. In the plant's first year, it
looks just like a carrot, producing a rosette of feathery
leaves, which when pulled up, will reveal a thick white
taproot that looks and smells like a small carrot.

The common Saint-John's-wort is another alien plant that
prospers in this field. It can be recognized by its paired
leaves and stems, and by the five-petaled yellow flowers
with conspicuous black dots on the margins of the petals.
In England, it was customary to hang a certain yellow-
blossomed plant in your window on the eve of Saint John's
Day (June 24), in order to ward off evil spirits. Eventually
the plant became known as Saint-John's-wort (wort
meaning plant or herb).

If you look toward the east (left) as you walk along the

mowed path, you will see a low hill in the distance. This 183-foot hill is Mount Holly, a remnant of a distinctive landform known as a cuesta. The cuesta was formed about 100 million years ago, while most of South Jersey was covered by the sea, when sediments laid down on the sea bottom became cemented together to form a long rocklike ridge. Other remnants trace the outline of this now-eroded ridge—the Highlands of the Navesink and Arney's Mount to the north, and Mount Laurel and Mullica Hill to the south.

The trail leaves the field and enters a plantation of coniferous trees, including our native white pine and three introduced species: Austrian pine, Norway spruce, and European larch. The trail then forks (near stake 11); bear left and follow it down the slope through a forest of oaks, holly, and dogwood. Further along, the trail reaches the outer edge of the floodplain, where a number of trees preferring moister soil are found: red maple, river birch, sour gum, and the conspicuous umbrella magnolia. Its large (eighteen-inch) dark green leaves crowded near the ends of the branches give this truly southern tree a tropical appearance. The umbrella magnolia's showy white flowers appear in May, and these give way to interesting-looking large brownish conelike fruit clusters in September.

The trail skirts a branch of Rancocas Creek for a short distance and then comes to a dead end at a backwater marsh of the creek. This spot offers a view of an extensive stand of wild rice, which thrives in the silty muck along the Rancocas. The rodlike seeds of this tall, plume-topped grass are a favorite food of a variety of ducks, among them pintail, blue-winged teal, and ring-necked, all of which can be seen here in the spring.

Another plant growing in this marsh, which is relished by many birds, is smartweed, of which there are half a dozen different species. All are recognized by their tight, spikelike clusters of tiny pink or whitish flowers and "knotted" stems with a papery sheath at each joint. Along with the many ducks a number of familiar songbirds—

Umbrella magnolia, Rancocas State Park

cardinals, redwing blackbirds, fox sparrows, song sparrows, and swamp sparrows—feed on smartweed seeds.

Backtrack to the point where you left the main trail (at stake 11), then bear left to follow this trail again. It winds through woods of sweet gum, black oak, and scattered tulip trees before reaching a huge sycamore tree. A short distance straight ahead (just beyond marker 18), look for a trail leading to the left; follow this trail down the hill and across a small creek, then turn right. The trail comes to another junction about 80 yards ahead; bear left here. This sandy footpath leads past oaks, American beech, and stands of mountain laurel. About $^1/_4$ mile from the junction, it enters a stand of Virginia pine. The Virginia pine is recognized by its short, twisted needles, which grow in bundles of two. Its squat appearance as a young tree and the fact that it rarely grows taller than forty to fifty feet combine to give this tree the alternative name of scrub pine. This stand of Virginia pine will yield eventually to deciduous forest like the type passed through earlier, since although it is an aggressive colonizer of abandoned fields, it cannot compete effectively in the long run with the broad-leaved trees.

Another $1/8$ mile further, the trail comes out to a black-top road. Turn right and follow this road over a creek, up a hill, and past some buildings. The road then comes out into an open area; turn right here and follow the trail toward the rightmost edge of the field. Along this section of the trail you may occasionally see a small brownish creature streak across the sand and up a nearby tree. This is the northern fence lizard, also known as the pine lizard, because of its frequent occurrence in open pine woods.

The trail reenters the woods to the right and then shortly passes into another open field. At the fork, follow the grassy path to the left along the edge of this field. Pass by the first entrance to the woods on the left and take the second entrance, which leads downhill at the far corner of the field. Follow the trail a few hundred yards to where you crossed the creek earlier, then bear left across the creek and return to the marked nature trail, turning left at marker 18. The trail passes through more upland woods before reaching another field.

Just before the trail reaches the parking area, it passes a large tree with black, checkered bark and glossy egg-shaped leaves. This is a persimmon tree, most easily recognized in the fall, when its small pumpkin-colored fruits dot the tree. The sweet, pulpy fruits, when ripe, are favored by deer, raccoons, and opossums, as well as people. Don't try tasting the green fruit though, or you'll really pucker up.

The Pine Barrens

Cranberry harvester, Lebanon State Park

22. Lebanon State Forest

Pakim Pond Area
Distance: 5 miles (Moderate)
Walking time: 2^1/2 hours
Directions: Take NJ 70 to NJ 72, then go southeast on NJ
72 for 1 mile and take the first entrance to Lebanon State
Forest. Go ^{3}/10 mile and turn right on the road to the
ranger's office. Follow this road 2 miles and then turn left
at the intersection and go about ^{1}/2 mile to the parking lot
by Pakim Pond. A parking fee is charged for day use
between Memorial Day and Labor Day. (609) 726-1191

The New Jersey Pine Barrens have always attracted
attention because of the region's rich human and natural
history; their precarious position today as a vast forest
wilderness in the midst of the nation's most densely
populated state has increased their appeal. Comprising
some 2,000 square miles, the area is the most extensive
tract of wildland in the northeast.

Though the flat, sandy expanses of pitch pine which
give the region its name are the typical image of the Pine
Barrens, the most noteworthy natural features are the wet
lowland swamps and bogs that crisscross the region. This
walk takes in a typical pitch pine barrens, as well as some
interesting lowland communities.

From the parking lot, walk through the picnic area near
Pakim Pond, and look for a pink-blazed trail which leads
left to a sand road. Bear right onto this sand road and
follow it for about a mile. The forest here is typical pitch
pine lowland forest, made up almost entirely of pitch pine,
whose irregularly arranged branches, scaly bark, and
gnarled trunk distinguish it from other pines found in New
Jersey. Black, blackjack, and post oaks are occasionally
scattered among the pines. Two other oaks are seen in the

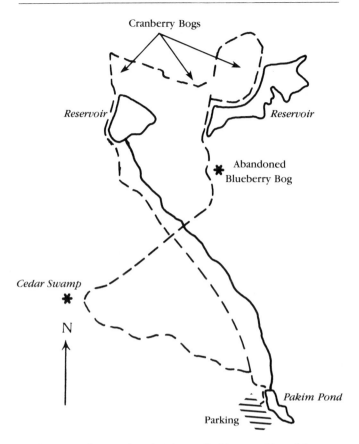

Cranberry Bogs

Reservoir

Reservoir

Abandoned
Blueberry Bog

Cedar Swamp

N

Pakim Pond

Parking

understory: the scrub oak (also called bear oak) and less
commonly, the dwarf chinquapin (or dwarf chestnut) oak.
Both of their names are descriptive of their size; neither of
these trees usually grows more than ten feet tall. The scrub
oak has oblong leaves with five to seven pointed lobes
separated by shallow sinuses, and twigs that are covered
with short brown fuzz. The dwarf chestnut oak has leaves
like those of the chestnut oak, but they are smaller and
have fewer teeth.

Shared by all of these trees is an ability to withstand the

extreme dryness of the sandy soil. Even though the region's annual precipitation is over forty inches, rainfall drains so rapidly through the porous sands that the water is largely unavailable to plants at the surface. This droughtiness makes for an extremely flammable forest, and fires of huge proportions are an almost annual occurrence in the Pine Barrens. The pitch pine is one of only three pines in the United States that responds to fire by sending forth sprouts, and invariably while walking one comes across pines with green crowns that have trunks still blackened by fire. The pitch pine not only tolerates fire, but is favored by it, since periodic blazes destroy the litter that accumulates on the forest floor. In time, this litter would prevent the establishment of young pine seedlings, eventually leading to an oak-dominated forest.

The sand road passes a gate and comes to a junction where it meets a narrower sand road; turn right here. Almost immediately a number of trees appear that hint there is water nearby: red maple, gray birch, sweet bay, sassafras, and sweet pepperbush. The first white cedars appear also, and shortly the road crosses Cooper Branch, one of three streams that join at Presidential Lakes before continuing west to empty into the Rancocas River. Another 300 yards further, the road forks; bear left onto another sand road.

The swamp forest disappears as quickly as it appeared, and again the trail leads through dry pine woods. The shrubs growing here are as well adapted to drought and fire as are the trees; sheep laurel and bracken fern, the most common shrubs, are especially vigorous after a fire. Sheep laurel, a close relative of the familiar mountain laurel, has small leathery, evergreen leaves which are pale green below.

The road passes a semiopen area on the right; this is a small blueberry plantation which has been abandoned for some time. The mounded rows of plants can still be seen, and in the fall a handful of berries can usually be harvested. It was at Whitesbog, just a few miles to the north, that the cultivated blueberry was developed by Elizabeth White in the early 1900s. In and around the Pine Barrens there are about 10,000 acres devoted to cultivated blueberry production, making New Jersey the nation's number-two producer of this crop.

At the end of the blueberry field bear left, and when you come to a fork, turn right to follow the edge of a large pond. In dry years the stumps of hundreds of white cedar trees stick up out of the mud, revealing that the pond is actually a cedar swamp that was cut over and flooded to serve as a reservoir. To the left of the road is a row of silver-barked hawthorn trees, and beyond it a young red cedar woodland which has developed on an abandoned cranberry bog.

Follow the trail along the edge of the pond, turning right at the far corner, until it passes back into the woods. Red-bellied and painted turtles slip from their pondside basking places into the tea-colored water as you walk past, and ducks and geese are commonly seen feeding further out. In summers when the reservoir is dry, herons step cautiously amid the cedar stumps, patiently searching the mud for their prey. Most common is the strikingly colored green heron. This small, dark heron has bright orange legs, a chestnut head and neck, a black crown, and a dark green back and wings.

After passing through woods for about ¼ mile, the road comes to a junction. Bear left and follow the road between two dormant cranberry bogs for a couple of hundred yards before turning right onto another sand road. This road passes a turnoff to the left, then comes to a T; bear right at this intersection and then immediately bear left. Like the reservoir seen earlier, the bog on your right was originally a white-cedar swamp probably cut over in the late nineteenth century and perhaps excavated for bog iron. It was this activity that led to the beginning of commercial cranberrying in the 1860s, when such bogs were turfed out by hand. Low dams like these were then built from the turf, after which wild cranberries from alongside nearby streams were transplanted into them. The bogs are flooded in autumn to permit harvest, and to keep cold winter winds from drying out the vines.

In the early days, cranberries were harvested by hand with many-tiered wooden scoops that pickers swung through the vines like large claws. Today, mechanical harvesting equipment has replaced the laborious hand methods of the past, and in summer or fall, one or more of the odd-looking harvesting machines can sometimes be seen resting alongside one of the dams.

Turn left where the road meets another intersection, and follow this for a few hundred yards through pine woods until it meets the intersection of two roads. Take the middle road, which leads along another shallow reservoir, and follow this past the reservoir and back into the woods. From here, follow this road $1/4$ mile to where it meets a larger sand road and turn left.

Occasionally while walking this road, you may run across one of the Pine Barrens' most distinctive animals, the northern pine snake. This large black and white snake spends much of its time burrowing in the soft sands, but sometimes moves about above ground. When disturbed, the pine snake makes itself conspicuous—striking out with its head, hissing loudly, and vibrating its tail. The entire display is convincing, yet there is little to fear, as the pine snake is not venomous.

The pine snake is one of three burrowing snakes whose distribution in New Jersey is limited almost exclusively to the soft sand of the Pine Barrens. The other two are the corn snake and the scarlet snake. The corn snake, the larger of the two, has a red or orange body which, in cross section, is shaped something like a slice of bread; that is, it has a distinctly flat belly, which meets the sides of its body at an angle. The third, the scarlet snake, is one of New Jersey's most beautiful snakes; it has a red head, and its more-rounded body is crossed by red saddles bordered by black.

The road reaches the junction where earlier you turned right to reach the cranberry bogs; turn right to follow the overgrown sand road for about 1/2 mile and then, just before the road rises into a large sandy area, bear left. Here the road skirts the edge of a cedar swamp, as can be seen from the red maples, young white cedars, and damp soil. In spring and summer this is a good place to listen for the loud, clear "tawee-tawee-tawee-tee-o" song of the hooded warbler. The male hooded warbler is one of the handsomest of the wood warbler family, with a bright yellow face and jet black hood. A number of other warblers nest in cedar and hardwood swamps throughout the New Jersey coastal plain; the black and white, black-throated green, and prothonotary warblers are among the most common.

Follow the trail 3/4 mile through more pine woods, merging with the pink-blazed Batona Trail along the way. This 39-mile trail was built by the Batona Hiking Club of Philadelphia in 1961. The trail leads into a sand road, on which you should bear left, and then back to the sand road you began on. After turning right onto this road, it is only a short walk back to the parking area.

23. Wharton State Forest

Batsto Village Area
Distance: 2 miles (Moderate)
Walking time: 2¹/₂ hours
Directions: Take the Garden State Parkway south to exit 52
(northbound exit 50). Go west on County Rd. 542 about
13 miles to the Batsto Historic Area. Park in the lot across
from the visitor center. A parking fee is charged during the
summer. (609) 561–3262

Two hundred years ago, Batsto was a dirty industrial
village where the blast furnace roared incessantly, smoke
filled the air, and water-powered mills turned out cornmeal and sawed boards to serve the needs of the town's
900 inhabitants. Today, Batsto is a quiet restored village
where the gristmill now stands silent, though the sawmill
cuts white cedar shingles for use in the maintenance of
Batsto's buildings. The Wharton State Forest headquarters
are located here, and were it not for this fact, Batsto would
have become one of the Pine Barrens' many vanished
towns.

The story of Batsto begins in 1766, when Charles Read
erected the Batsto Furnace and began producing kettles,
skillets, stoves, and a variety of other iron products. In
1770, Col. John Cox, assistant quartermaster general of the
Continental Army, acquired control of the ironworks, and
began casting cannon and cannonballs for use against the
British during the Revolutionary War. Later, the furnace
would also furnish munitions for the War of 1812, water
pipe for New York City, and the steam cylinder for one of
John Fitch's experimental steamboats.

Competition from Pennsylvania furnaces using easier to
obtain mineral ore eventually forced the Batsto Furnace to
close in 1848, but as the iron industry died, a new one was

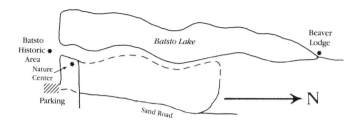

born—glass manufacturing. Using the white Pine Barrens'
sand as its principal raw material, the Batsto glassworks
produced flat glass for windows and street lamps. Many of
the gas lamps that lighted the streets of New York and
Philadelphia during the latter part of the nineteenth
century contained Batsto glass.

Begin your walk with a tour of Batsto; a trail map which
identifies the various buildings in the village can be
obtained at the visitor's center. Batsto Furnace and the
glassworks are no longer standing, but as you walk
through the village, you will see signs of their former
presence. Half-buried in the sand are fragments of seashells
brought here from the coast for use as flux in the furnace.
The shells were introduced to purify the iron, as the
calcium carbonate in them combined with impurities to
form a slag which floated on top of the molten iron. Pieces
of this slag can also be seen scattered about, and thousands
of pieces of glass, in hues of green, blue, and amber, attest
to the previous existence of the glass factory.

To begin the trail walk, follow the road that leads to the
Nature Center. Just beyond the center, where the road
bends to the right, there is a trail (much of which is a
narrow path through the encroaching bushes) on the left-
hand side; begin here. At the entrance to the trail are some
large pieces of bog iron, which was the type of iron ore
used at the Batsto Furnace.

Bog iron is formed when rainwater that has leached iron

from the sands moves underground into nearby streams and then oxidizes on contact with the air. The oxidized iron forms a rusty-colored scum on the surface which drifts over to the bank of the stream, where it permeates the sands and gravels to such an extent that it forms an iron-sandstone composite like the rocks here. Batsto ore raisers would skim the bog iron from the surface of streams or dig it from the banks, then haul it overland to the furnace in wagons or by water in long, flat-bottomed ore boats.

The trail enters a stretch of typical Pine Barrens woods—pitch pine and black oak with a lower layer of blueberry, huckleberry, and sheep laurel shrubs—and continues a short distance before reaching the junction of two marked trails. Take the left trail, which has a yellow over red blaze. To the right of the trail here are several sweet bay magnolias which mark the edge of a small cedar swamp. The sweet bay is a small tree with thick, leathery, elliptic leaves which smell spicy when crushed. Wherever the sweet bay is seen in the Pine Barrens, it is certain that there is ample water nearby. Along this trail it often grows beside the small streams that run down into Batsto Lake.

Another $1/4$ mile further the trail forks again; follow the left-hand trail, which is marked by a yellow blaze. This trail continues to provide beautiful views upstream toward the northern end of Batsto Lake, which is usually full even in times of prolonged drought. This is because the enormous volume of groundwater beneath the sandy soil continually recharges the surface stream, ponds, and bogs of the Pine Barrens.

The water in Batsto Lake, and in most of the rivers and lakes of the Pine Barrens, is a dark tea color. This is caused by the combination of tannins leached from nearby cedar trees and iron from the groundwater. Despite its unappealing color, Pine Barrens water is remarkably pure. A century ago, sea captains took Pine Barrens "cedar

Joseph Wharton mansion, Batsto Village

water" with them on voyages, since it would remain sweet longer than any other water available to them.

At the upper reaches of Batsto Lake, where the pine woods begin to give way to a large white cedar swamp, there has been a good deal of beaver activity. Beavers cut down trees for three reasons: for food, for building their lodge and dam, and to keep their continually growing teeth worn down. Although they prefer the bark of trees like poplar, birch, and willow as food, here in the Pine Barrens they make do with scrub oak, white cedar, and pitch pine.

It is on one of the small white cedar islands that the beavers have built their low conical lodge of sticks and mud. Inside the lodge is a chamber which is connected with the outside by a number of tunnels that open underwater. In winter, the beavers store saplings under the water near the lodge, and they can leave the lodge via these tunnels and return to their chamber with some of the saplings for food.

Wharton State Forest 175

Along certain sections of this trail are two shrubs that are typical of lowland areas in the Pine Barrens: sweet pepperbush and fetterbush, or swamp sweetbells. Both of these shrubs have thin, fine-toothed leaves; however, those of the sweet pepperbush are short pointed and those of the fetterbush long pointed. Sweet pepperbush is also distinguished by its hairy twigs, which are held erect, and by the fact that it often occurs in colonies, as it is one of the few shrubs that may reproduce by means of underground runners. Both plants have very fragrant flowers, the fetterbush blooming in mid-May, the sweet pepperbush in late summer.

Another plant seen along this part of the trail is turkeybeard. A member of the lily family, turkeybeard is identified by its tall stalk supporting a cluster of white flowers that arise from a tussock of long, grasslike leaves. Turkeybeard is unusual in that its range is largely restricted to mountain woods of the southern Appalachians, yet it emerges onto the Coastal Plain briefly in Delaware and occurs commonly here in the Pine Barrens, where it reaches its northern limit. There are over 100 other plants which, like turkeybeard, reach their northern geographic limit in the Pine Barrens. At the same time, there are at least 21 species of northern plants that reach their southern limit here, making the Pine Barrens the region with the greatest overlap in plant ranges of eastern North America.

Early in the evenings beginning in late April one can hear carpenter frogs calling from the sedge hummocks along the edge of the lake. The carpenter frog gets its name from its call, which sounds like two carpenters hitting nails one right after the other. Large choruses sound like a whole construction crew hammering away.

Though easily heard, the carpenter frog is harder to see, as it is only about two inches long, and its brownish color blends perfectly with the tannin-stained water. Its occurrence in the Pine Barrens is interesting, since it is at its northern limit here, and yet it often outnumbers more widely distributed frogs such as the spring peeper, chorus frog, and wood frog. This is because the carpenter frog has adapted to the extremely acidic water of the Pine Barrens' streams and bogs. Its eggs, and also those of the lovely Pine Barrens tree frog, can survive in water where the pH is as low as 4.0 (7.0 is neutral).

The trail eventually swings away from the water's edge and leads out onto a sand road. The fine white sand along this road is only barely covered by vegetation in many places, mostly lichens and patches of downy hudsonia, also known as golden heather. Golden heather is a moss-like shrub that has short, needlelike leaves and small yellow flowers that spill out over the sands in late spring. Follow this road about $^1/_4$ mile until it meets another sand road and then bear right. The woods here are dominated by black oak rather than pitch pine, although the pitch pine is still common, and they are somewhat sparser than the pine forest traveled through earlier.

It is hard to tell today, but all of these forests have been cut repeatedly to produce charcoal which fueled the fires of the Batsto Furnace. To make charcoal, colliers—as the men who made charcoal were called—stacked cordwood cut from the nearby forest into ten- to twenty-foot-high vertical stacks and then covered the wood with pieces of sandy turf. This turf covering kept the wood from burning too quickly by cutting off the supply of oxygen to the fire. The colliers dropped burning kindling into a hole in the top of the mound and sealed it over. They kept watch over it day and night for a week or more, carefully regulating the air supply by opening and closing vents in the mound, until the wood was evenly charred. Finally, carters hauled the charcoal by wagon to the furnace, whose roar they could most likely hear as they came over the sand roads.

After about $^3/_4$ mile, the road reaches a junction marked by a wooden fence on the right. The sand here is littered with refuse from Batsto's earlier days: slag, charcoal, pieces of bog iron, and even scraps of finished iron. Go past the fence and follow the road to the left back to the parking lot.

Wharton State Forest 177

The Atlantic Coast

Lighthouse, Atlantic coast

24. Gateway National Recreation Area

Sandy Hook
Distance: 5^1/$_2$ miles (Moderate)
Walking time: 3 hours
Directions: Take the Garden State Parkway to exit 117. Go east on NJ 36 toward Highlands. After crossing the Highlands bridge, bear right and follow signs to park entrance. Proceed past entrance and go 2 miles to the visitor center parking lot (on right). A parking fee of $4.00 on weekdays and $5.00 on weekends and holidays is charged from Memorial Day weekend through Labor Day.
(908) 872-0115

Because it dominates a major channel into New York harbor, Sandy Hook has been the site of lighthouses, forts, and weapons emplacements since the earliest of colonial times. As early as 1687, Sandy Hook was considered extremely important to the defense of New York City. In that year, the royal governor of New York offered a plan that would "make up a small Fort with twelve guns upon Sandy Hook, the channel there being so near the shore that no vessel can go in or out but she must come so near the Point that from on board ship one might toss a biscuit cake on shore."

Sandy Hook's uniqueness lies not only in its rich history, but also in its natural environment of holly forests, fresh- and saltwater marshes, sand dunes, and scores of migrating birds. As with most of the shore walks described in this book, this one is more enjoyable in the fall or early spring, when hot weather, mosquitoes, and crowds can be avoided.

You may wish to stop at the Spermaceti Cove Visitor Center before you begin your walk. The building, which originally served as a lifesaving station, houses a variety of

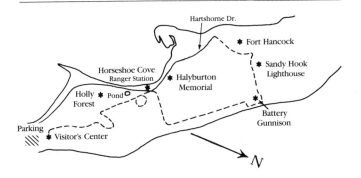

Hartshorne Dr.

✳ Fort Hancock

✳ Sandy Hook
Lighthouse

Horseshoe Cove
Ranger Station   ✳ Halyburton
Memorial

Holly ✳ Pond ○
Forest

Battery
Gunnison

Parking
✳ Visitor's Center

N

exhibits on the history and natural history of Sandy Hook.
From the visitor center, follow the road that loops around
the center back to the parking area and look for the "Old
Dune Trail" sign on the right. This trail weaves through the
backdune area, which has been stabilized by the growth of
various plants. At the entrance to the trail some of these
plants can be seen: poison ivy, seaside goldenrod, beach
heather, and bayberry. Found here, though less common
elsewhere on the dunes, is the groundsel-tree. Actually a
shrub, the groundsel-tree is recognized by its small white
silky flowers and fruits and its thick gray green leaves.
These leaves can be confusing, as those on the upper part
of the plant are small and often lack teeth, while those on
the lower part are larger and wedge shaped, and have
large teeth. The groundsel-tree is more commonly found in
the upper margins of coastal salt marshes.

   Though small and usually hugging the sand, the prickly
pear cactus growing here is hard to overlook. In summer it
boasts showy yellow flowers, and these give way to
purplish red fruits in the fall. These pulpy fruits are edible,
but be sure to remove the spines first. Covering the thick,
fleshy skins as well as the fruits, these spines are actually
modified leaves which protect the plant from herbivorous
animals. The spines do not keep all animals away, however, and many prickly pear cacti can be found with teeth

marks along the stem. This is the work of the cottontail rabbit who obtains water from the succulent stem.

After crossing a small asphalt road, the trail comes to a grove of holly trees. This grove is actually part of the large holly forest that covers much of the bay side of this portion of Sandy Hook. This is one of the most extensive stands of American holly along the Atlantic coast and has been set aside as a natural area for scientific research. Many of the trees in the natural area are over 100 years old, and the oldest is approximately 150 years old. Where the trail forks within the grove, bear right.

After emerging from the holly grove, you pass many bleached red cedar snags—standing dead trees from which most of the leaves and limbs have fallen. These have been killed by salt spray, which limits the growth of all the trees close to the ocean beach. It has been found that plant growth is limited to a level below a fifteen-degree line drawn from the water's edge; this level is known as the salt-spray horizon.

The trail heads left and soon crosses an old dirt road. From 1874 to 1919, all testing of army guns took place at the Sandy Hook Proving Ground, and although an extensive search has been conducted, the possibility exists that some live artillery shells are still buried in the dunes. Many of the old roads here date back to that era, when they linked together an extensive ammunition storage complex.

The trail then comes upon a small freshwater pond, visible from the observation deck on the left. This pond actually began as a saltwater lagoon which became separated from the salt water of ocean and bay by shifting sands. Over the years rainfall has formed a layer of fresh water on top of the salt water that remained in the pond. Since fresh-water is not as heavy as salt water, they do not mix, and an important freshwater habitat was created. Here painted turtles, green frogs, ducks, and marsh hawks have a home in an otherwise dry and forbidding landscape.

American holly, Gateway National Recreation Area

As the trail begins to curve around, it passes a former Nike-Hercules missile site. The once electrified fence surrounding the site now serves as a perch for scores of migrating songbirds in the spring and fall. Because it is located along the Atlantic flyway, the major path of bird migration in the eastern United States, a wide variety of migrants can be seen at Sandy Hook. The birds tend to concentrate along Sandy Hook before and after crossing the open-water expanse of New York Bay. Most numerous are myrtle warblers, which can be seen foraging for the berries of bayberry, red cedar, and poison ivy. Though the

Gateway National Recreation Area 183

fall and spring migrations bring as many as twenty or more species of warbler to Sandy Hook, the myrtle is easily recognized, as it is the only yellow-rumped warbler with a white throat.

Continue to the right on the sandy trail, which curves back around to join the dirt road again; follow it away from the beach out to the ranger station on the main road (Hartshorne Drive) and turn right. The road partially follows the old bed of the New Jersey Southern Railroad, which once extended to the northern tip of Horseshoe Cove, where there was a steamboat landing. In fall, one often finds exhausted monarch butterflies along the side of the road. Monarchs follow much the same path as migrating birds and are often seen on Sandy Hook. You may also see an occasional box turtle along the road here.

After about a mile, the road passes the turnoff to North Beach, leads uphill, and soon comes to the Halyburton Monument, which was erected in memory of Lieut. Hamilton Douglas-Halyburton. Shortly after the Revolutionary War had ended, the ships of the Royal Navy were at anchor in Sandy Hook Bay while waiting to evacuate the British army from New York City. While anchored there, a small group of seamen deserted one of the ships, the HMS *Assistance.* Lieutenant Halyburton and thirteen members of his crew went after them in a small boat, but were caught in a sudden blizzard. Halyburton and his men were later found frozen to death and were buried somewhere on Sandy Hook. A monument was erected but was destroyed by vandals, and the site was lost until 1908 when railroad workers digging for the new railroad line uncovered the old burial vault.

As you pass the salt marsh on Horseshoe Cove, look out to the northern point of the cove. This is one of the barbs that make Sandy Hook such a distinctive landform. When viewed on a map, South Island and the northern tip of Spermaceti Cove similarly appear as barbs, while the tip of the sand spit forms the hook. These formations are clues to the geologic processes that have created Sandy Hook.

Sandy Hook began as a small sandbar formed from shell fragments and sediments. The alongshore current, moving north along the coast, deposited more sand on the bar until it became an island. Too weak to maintain a continuous line, the current that produced the island swung westward into an embayment, thus forming a hook (South Island). Sea Bright, the barrier beach to the south of the island, extended northward via the same process to connect with the hook, forming what geologists call a sand spit. With the shallowing of the water by the growth of the spit, the current gradually resumed its straight course until it again turned inward to form a second barb— Spermaceti Cove. The process repeated itself again to form Horseshoe Cove, and it is only periodic dredging that has prevented Sandy Hook from growing in this manner out into the shipping channel leading to New York City.

Another $1/8$ mile further, where the road forks, bear right and follow the road to the entrance to Fort Hancock. Fort Hancock and its gun batteries were constructed during the 1890s to protect the entrance to New York harbor. Once a bustling army town of hundreds of officers, enlisted men, and their families, Fort Hancock is now a strange ghost town. Barracks, mess halls, and other buildings stand empty, and grass grows up out of the brick paths.

Enter the parade ground, which is flanked by enlisted men's barracks on the right and officers' quarters on the left. The officers' quarters, which appear to be a bit neglected now, were stately homes built for the married officers of the coast artillery. The largest house, in the middle of the row, was the commanding officer's. In the summer, the houses are used by nonprofit organizations such as scouting groups and community centers.

At the end of the parade ground, turn right and follow the road to the guard house, which now serves as the

Sandy Hook Museum. A variety of historic photographs and artifacts are exhibited here, some housed in the original jail cells. From the museum, head for the light-house, which can be seen just a short distance away.

Constructed by the colony of New York to reduce shipping losses on the outer shoals of Sandy Hook, Sandy Hook lighthouse is the oldest lighthouse in the United States and has been in operation since 1764. Though originally built only 500 feet from the end of the hook, the lighthouse today is about one and one-half miles away, because the end of the sand spit has been built up by alongshore currents.

From the lighthouse, follow Magruder Road back toward the fort entrance, but turn left almost immediately onto Gunnison Road. Follow it out to Battery Gunnison, a concrete artillery battery that was erected in 1904. Here two six-inch-caliber guns, as well as the surrounding parapets, the tunnels connecting the cartridge rooms, and a mechanical cartridge-lifting machine can still be seen. From the top of the battery there is an excellent view of the Manhattan skyline and the rest of New York City.

To return, you may wish to walk along the beach; however, a large portion is closed during the summer to protect nesting shorebirds. The other route is to walk back through the fort to Hartshorne Drive, turn left, and follow it back to the visitor center.

25. Allaire State Park

Distance: Including village part, 3 miles (Easy)
Walking time: 2 hours
Directions: From Interstate 195 take exit 31B onto County Rd. 547 North. Take an immediate right at the traffic light onto 524 East. Follow the signs $1^1/4$ miles to the Main Entrance (just past the Park Office) and take this road to the large parking lot adjacent to Allaire Village. The park and village are open daily 8 A.M. to 8 P.M. from Memorial Day to Labor Day and 8 A.M. to 4:30 P.M. off season. The historic buildings in the village are open daily 10 A.M. to 5 P.M. from May 1 to Labor Day, on weekends only in September and October, and are closed the rest of the year. A parking fee of $4.00 on weekdays and $5.00 on weekends is charged from May to September, as is a village admission fee of $2.00 for adults and $1.00 for children. The portion of this walk within the restored village is accessible to wheelchairs and strollers. Park Office: (908) 938-2371; Village Office: (908) 938-2253.

In the southeastern corner of Monmouth County, the Manasquan River winds through an old Indian ceremonial area that has been known since before 1650 as Squankum. The river's floodplain provides a wetland environment where many varieties of plant life somewhat uncommon so near the ocean have found a congenial home. The moistness of the area also facilitates the natural and ongoing process through which iron oxides seep into the swamps and eventually produce iron ore. The extraction of this ore for use in the mechanized production of iron products changed the face, and the mood, of this and many other locations to the south, at least for a time, and helped replace the rhythms of ancient sacred ceremonies with the rituals of modern industrial life. This walk takes

187

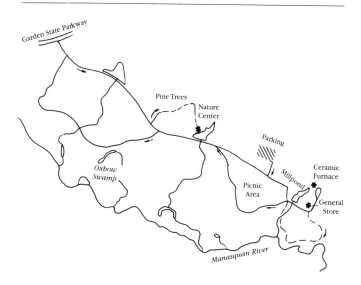

you on a tour through the restored village of Allaire, once
a thriving center of the bog iron industry, and then
through some of the natural habitat surrounding the
village.

The clamor of industry first broke the stillness of this
site, originally known as Williamsburg Forge and then as
Monmouth Furnace, around the turn of the nineteenth
century. In 1822 Benjamin Howell, a Philadelphia business-
man, began operating the furnace, which later that year
was purchased by James P. Allaire, who renamed the
operation the Howell Works. Allaire was a very successful
brass founder who built engines and other mechanical
parts for steamships, including the brass air chamber for
Robert Fulton's *Clermont,* in his New York City plant. The
Howell Works flourished under Allaire's supervision and
provided pig iron and castings for his engine shop in the
city, as well as a variety of housewares and utensils for
both local and metropolitan markets.

Begin your walk at the Visitor Center, which is in the

Casting house stack, Allaire Village

near end of the long building to the right of the snack bar and restrooms. The center houses displays on the natural and human history of the area, on the career of James Allaire, on the iron production process, and on the efforts of businessmen, Boy Scouts, the state, and non-profit organizations such as Allaire Village, Inc., all of whom have been involved in the restoration work. This building is typical of the brick row houses that Allaire built as dwellings for the four hundred or more inhabitants of the village.

From the Visitor Center follow the sidewalk to the right, around the back of the building, and across the grassy area to the church. The bell for this church was made here at the Howell Works, being placed at the rear of the building because the front portion was constructed some years earlier and was considered unable to support such a weight. On weekdays the church also served as a school, with the minister frequently assuming the task of teacher and receiving an annual salary of about five hundred dollars for these combined duties.

Bear right at the church and follow the road past the small brick foreman's cottage, complete with iron windowsills and thresholds, which was built in 1827 and was the first of such buildings constructed by Allaire. At the bottom of the hill, go left along the end of the millpond, where fishing privileges are reserved for children under fourteen years of age. The gristmill, which was located just across the path from the pond, turned the crops from Allaire's five farms into freshly ground wheat flour and cornmeal. And the bakery, the two-story building with more ironwork trim just beyond the pond on the left, produced bread and other baked goods for the community, since the individual homes provided by Allaire did not contain ovens.

Continue past the blacksmith's shop. Where the main path turns left take the smaller path down the hill to the

General store, Allaire Village

right. This path leads around to a rather impressive view of the central stack of the former blast furnace and casting house. Here the iron ore was smelted and formed into the shapes of pots, pans, pipes, kettles, stoves, and various other items. Allaire had purchased 8,000 acres of the surrounding woodland to ensure an adequate supply of fuel to satisfy the enormous appetite of the furnace, which devoured fifty cords of wood, in the form of charcoal, during a twenty-four-hour period. This added up each year to a pile of wood eight feet wide, four feet high, and five miles long. Retrace your steps back to the main path and stop at the general store, the large stone building on the corner.

This store was a bustling shopping center not only for the Howell Works community, but also for the population of the surrounding region. It benefited as well from the fact that the village was the last stop before Perth Amboy on the stagecoach route from Toms River. Allaire conducted both retail and wholesale trade here, and in its best years the store's volume of business rivaled that of some New York City establishments. The superintendent often boasted that he could satisfy the demands of any customer with what he had in stock. Today the store offers a somewhat more limited line of craft items and gifts.

The general store continued operating even after the fires in the furnace were finally extinguished in 1848, due to the discovery of higher-grade ore in Pennsylvania and the more efficient production of iron products through the use of coal. With the failure of the industrial heart of the Howell Works, the vitality of the village gradually drained away. For over a quarter of a century, though, it flourished as a relatively self-contained community in which the farmers, millers, bakers, a wide variety of craft workers, the minister, and teacher played vital roles. The village also had its own post office, as well as its own currency— copper coins and engraved notes that ranged in value from six and a quarter cents to ten dollars. And often on summer evenings many residents would trade their tools for musical instruments and play in the outdoor concerts given by the community orchestra.

Continue along past the carpenter shop and then the white brick enameling furnace, which is to the left of the loop that marks the end of the village road. Think of the din that must have marked this village when both the blast furnace and this enameling furnace were in operation. The gentler sounds of the village—people talking, birds singing, the movement of the gristmill's wheel, the tintinnabulation of the smithy's anvil chorus—would have been obliterated by the roar. One wonders how the people who lived in the village coped with this noise: did they stop up their ears or simply tune it out, so that it became part of the unnoticed background?

To continue your village tour with a walk through the neighboring woods, circle back past the general store and turn left onto the path you followed before to see the blast furnace. The yellow-blazed trail drops down onto the floodplain immediately, and a sign tells of the conditions ahead—wet and muddy. The trail may be completely impassable after heavy rains, but even when it is very soggy, it is worth getting your feet wet to experience the floodplain environment. But be careful, since you may begin to speed up your pace, thinking that the soil is dry enough not to cause a spill. It is best to almost tiptoe on such soil, which is fine, since it slows you down to a rhythm which is more in keeping with the undulation of the river. The first sensation you may notice after the slippery feeling underfoot is the silty smell in the air, a smell continually replenished by the silt-laden Manasquan River. The river's clay banks and lack of any midstream obstacles save a few partially submerged trees give it a particularly muted voice, even when swollen in the spring.

The trail loops back around to leave the floodplain near the millpond spillway, which brings a new sound to your ears. The rushing water creates "white noise," which has a noticeably soothing, quieting effect on the body. As you walk, the white noise of the spillway diminishes, to be replaced by a different sort of white noise, that of the wind through the trees. Bear left along the rail fence, then where the road forks near the vertical sawmill site, you may follow either path. Both lead through a picnic area before joining a green-blazed trail which parallels the mill raceway. Turn left onto this path, and notice how different the sound of your steps is on the gravelly path from that of the floodplain.

You will shortly pass a small pond on the right, where you should keep an ear out for tree swallows, whose voice has a strangely mechanical quality. It's likely that such a voice evolved to meet the unique acoustical needs of a bird that spends so much of its time darting and dashing above the surface of water. Continue to where a red-blazed trail leads to the left, past an open area on the right dotted with a few young white oaks. This area has a distinctly different "keynote"—the characteristic sound it

Allaire State Park 193

produces—from the areas you have traversed so far. The rustle of grasses is joined in winter by the deeper rustle of the dry oak leaves, which remain on the branches through the quiet season.

As the path bends to the right, listen closely. Do you hear ducks quacking? In the woods on both sides of the trail are small breeding pools (formed in an old oxbow of the river) where after the first March rains, wood frogs, whose voice resembles a duck, congregate to breed. See how close you can approach the frogs before they hear (actually *feel*) you and stop calling. If you've gotten close to the water, you'll likely see skunk cabbage flowers emerging from the warming soil, and if you visit the ponds a few weeks after the first rains, you can spot jellylike masses of wood frog eggs attached to submerged branches or vegetation. They become easier to spot over time, as there is a green algae that grows in the egg mass and gets darker as the tadpoles develop inside.

Now as the wood frog voices recede, you'll hear a different form of white noise from the one heard in the village—the sound of cars and trucks rushing by on Interstate 195. Though the sound is distinctly noticeable now, it's been "in the air" from the beginning of your walk, as much a part of the unnoticed background as the furnaces must have been a century and a half ago. We have granted to our automobiles the same dispensation that was granted to Benjamin Howell and James Allaire—the dispensation to make noise. Once that power was granted only to the Church. The bell that rang out from the village church steeple signaled the divine, saying "Listen! God!" as bells had done all around the world for thousands of years. It was in the era of the Howell Works that people first granted to industrialists the right to interrupt the sacred silence, and that right has yet to be revoked. We are surrounded by the steady drone of the internal combustion engine.

In the Lenape village of Squankum, sacred silence was

the keynote. It was so present that it was taken for granted. To break the silence was also a sacred activity. The shaman's name in Lenape—*meteu*—came from the voice of his drum, which said, and was thus called, *meteohet*. Like the church bell, the drum spoke in rich and resonant overtones, a fact which the onomatopoeic renderings of both of their sounds—"ring-g-g" and *"meteohet"*—capture. Both sounds begin abruptly, spread out and resound, then are silent again. The sanctity of both sounds, however, could only exist in a world where silence was a commonplace.

Where the trail rejoins the green-blazed raceway trail, turn right and continue until you almost reach the place where you first turned off. Follow the path that leads left over the raceway and then immediately bear right to enter a little pitch pine/hardwood forest. The keynote changes here, both above where the wind moves through the pine boughs, and below, with the sound of your feet padding against the fallen pine needles. Turn right where the trail meets another woods road, and follow it a short distance to where you can see the log building ahead. This is the Nature Center, where you may wish to stop and have lunch (there is a nice picnic area in front next to the pond). From the Nature Center, follow the concrete walk (or the raceway trail) back to the parking lot.

26. Island Beach State Park

Distance: $3^1/_2$ miles (Moderate)
Walking time: 2 hours
Directions: Take the Garden State Parkway to exit 82.
Then take NJ 37 east to NJ 35 south. Go past park entrance
and continue to parking lot A-8. The parking fee is $6.00
on weekdays and $7.00 on weekends and holidays from
Memorial Day to Labor Day, and $4.00 off season. During
the summer, an additional $1.00 toll is charged at the
guardhouse just before lot A-8. (908) 793–0506

As one of the last natural expanses of barrier beach along
the Atlantic shore, Island Beach State Park is truly worth a
visit. While all of New Jersey's other barrier islands have
undergone extensive development, this ten-mile strip
remains in its natural state. It is a fragile strip which owes
its existence to the ocean, and yet the ocean constantly
threatens to destroy it.

Because most of the park has been set aside as a botanical preserve, there are no extensive trails. An interesting
walk can, however, be created by walking the series of
trails that lead from the road out to the ocean beaches.
Because these beaches are flooded with people during the
summer, this walk is best if taken after Labor Day. (The
parking fee is reduced then also.)

From parking lot A-8, follow the path that leads to the
beach. Immediately you enter a thicket of low-growing
shrubs and trees. The most obvious plant is American
holly, joined by wild cherry and shadbush. Almost as soon
as you have entered this thicket, you leave it behind, and
come to the top of the foredune, the dune closest to the
beach. From here you can see the ocean in front of you
and still look back to see Barnegat Bay behind.

There is a noticeable increase in the force of the wind as

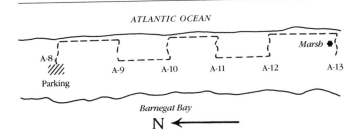

ATLANTIC OCEAN

A-8
Parking
A-9 A-10 A-11 A-12 A-13

Marsh

Barnegat Bay

N ←

one climbs to the top of the dune, and it is the wind that is responsible for much of the lay of the land of the barrier beach. The wind picks up sand from the beach and deposits it on the dunes behind. Over time, a series of dunes like the ones visible from this rise is created.

As you continue toward the beach, the vegetation becomes sparse, consisting mainly of beach grass (also called dune grass or marram grass). Beach grass is the anchor that holds the dunes against the effects of wind and wave. Each plant has horizontal stems that creep along the sand, sending up new tufts of leaves and roots every few inches. This network of roots help to bind the sand in place, stabilizing the dune and building it higher.

In order to grow here, the beach grass must be able to survive the salt spray the wind carries with it. Only a very few plants are as tolerant of the salt spray as the beach grass, and these can be found in smaller numbers along the trail here. Most noticeable is the seaside goldenrod, with its narrow, fleshy leaves and yellow blossoms arranged in a graceful plume. If you look closely, you can see that the succulent leaves are protected by a waxy coating which helps the plant conserve moisture. Less conspicuous is the dusty miller, a low, matted plant with deeply lobed leaves that are covered with white hairs. These hairs reflect the strong sun and also provide the leaves with vital insulation from the wind and salt spray.

Continue out to the beach and turn right. In the fall, when the bluefish are running, fishermen are lined up along this beach. About 200 yards up the beach, turn right to follow the path to the next parking area. After passing the foredune again, you come to an area where the dunes have been broken by the wind into a jumble of low dunes, hollows, and broad flat swales. This area is known as the primary backdune.

Beyond the backdune area you enter a shrub thicket again. On either side of the trail can be seen the layer of leaf litter that has been built upon the top of the sand. It may seem strange that the wild cherry and American holly trees here are only growing to the same height as the blueberry and bayberry bushes. This is because the salt spray is carried back this far and kills any growth above the level of the windstream that crosses the barrier island.

After the trail emerges at parking lot A-9, turn left to follow the road. This stretch of hard ground is a relief from the soft sands of the beach and dunes. You may notice that plants found closer to the beach are also found along this road, but that they grow taller here. This is because the road lies just beyond the reach of the harshest winds and salt spray. Conditions are even less harsh on the bay side of the road, where the dunes support patches of woodland made up of red cedars, holly, wild cherry, pitch pine, and a few other trees.

Just before you reach the next parking area, you pass on the left a holly tree laden with red berries. In holly trees, the male and female flowers occur on separate trees, and only the female trees, like this one, bear fruit. The berries can be found on female trees in almost every month of the year, and thus are an important source of food for many birds.

Another holly marks the beginning of the trail from parking lot A-10. Though the trunk of this tree is only about ten inches in diameter, the tree may be as much as 125 years old. Continue toward the beach, where before reaching the foredune, the trail passes a large patch of Virginia creeper sprawled across the sand. This plant is

Seaside goldenrod, Island Beach State Park

easily recognized by its compound leaves consisting of five leaflets arranged like spokes of a wheel. In the fall, these leaves turn to crimson, and with its blue fruits, the Virginia creeper becomes one of the most colorful plants on the dunes.

Many of the low backdunes along here are covered with hudsonia, or beach heather. Because it is not very tolerant of salt spray, the beach heather tends to grow behind the foredunes in areas that are too dry to support the growth of larger plants. Its small yellow flowers dot the sands in early summer.

Again, the trail leaves the shelter of the backdunes and emerges into the foredune area. Where the trail reaches the top of the foredune, stop for a moment to look out over a sea of beach grass. At certain times in the fall, you can stand and watch as wave upon wave of migrating tree swallows skim the top of the grass. As many as a thousand or more may pass as you stand, their iridescent green backs and white bellies flashing in the sun as they go by.

After the trail emerges onto the beach again, turn right. Note that sections of the drift fence along the front of the foredune have been buried by sand carried off the beach by the wind. With so much sand constantly being taken from the beach, why does it remain?

New sand is constantly being added to the beach, deposited by the alongshore currents which sweep southward. The sand being deposited here is coming from around Long Branch and Asbury, where coastal bluffs are being severely eroded by the ocean waves. The quantity of sand carried by the alongshore currents diminishes southward, so that New Jersey's southernmost barrier beaches are much smaller and more broken up than those to the north, like Island Beach.

Leave the beach along the trail to parking lot A-ll; this trail is marked by a sign and a huge blow-out—an area where the dune has largely disappeared. Although small blow-outs occur fairly often during fierce storms, they are repaired as vegetation quickly colonizes the blow-out and begins again the process of dune building. This one, however, has probably been aggravated by constant walking along the path, as the plants necessary to rebuild the dune cannot get a footing because of the trampling. This is why it is so important to stay off the dunes and remain on the designated trails.

After emerging at lot A-11, turn left along the road, which is flanked on the right by an impenetrable thicket of greenbrier. Most people have had at least one unpleasant encounter with this prickly vine. When viewed from this safe distance in the fall, the greenbrier thicket is a colorful jumble of yellow leaves and green stems. Another colorful plant along the road is dwarf or winged sumac, which has fire-red leaves in autumn. In other seasons, winged sumac is easily recognized by its large leaves which are divided into eleven to twenty-three narrow, shining leaflets. The main vein of the leaves, called the midrib, gives the shrub its name, as it is bordered by thin wings.

At parking lot A-12, follow the path once more to the beach, then turn right again and continue to the next path back through the dunes. Before reaching the road, the trail comes upon a distinctly different area, where you can see the tall feathery plumes of phragmites or reed grass, along with scattered red maple trees. At first, both seem out of place in this arid environment. Further along, the trail reveals that you have come upon a freshwater marsh. Along the short section of boardwalk can be seen marsh fern, royal fern, and even sphagnum moss when the water level is low. This marsh is a low-lying area that exposes the underlying groundwater table of Island Beach, which lies well below the surface in most sections of the barrier island.

Just beyond the boardwalk, the trail emerges at parking area A-13. From here, you may turn right and return via the road, or if your legs are up to it, walk out to the beach and walk by the water.

Island Beach State Park 201

27. Edwin B. Forsythe National Wildlife Refuge

Distance: 8 miles (Moderate)
Walking time: 4 hours
Directions: Take the Garden State Parkway to exit 48, then go south on US 9 for 6 miles to Oceanville. Look for the sign on the right-hand side of the road, which marks the refuge entrance to the left. Follow the road to the refuge headquarters and park there. (609) 652–1665

Walking the auto tour at the Brigantine division of the Edwin B. Forsythe National Wildlife Refuge might at first seem crazy—the eight-mile loop is along a level dirt road often crowded with cars. However, the spectacle of tens of thousands of geese and ducks continuously moving back and forth across the sky completely diverts one's attention from the activity on the ground. Also, if you begin at dawn, when the refuge opens, you will only have to share the road with a few hardy birdwatchers.

The refuge, which consists of 20,000 acres of tidal marsh, freshwater pools, and saltwater bays and channels, was established in 1939 for the protection and management of migratory waterfowl. The area is a major stopping point along the Atlantic flyway, as well as being an important wintering area for as many as 150,000 geese, ducks, and other birds. Except for summer, when mosquitoes and greenhead flies are biting, the Edwin B. Forsythe National Wildlife Refuge is a spectacular place to visit year round. March and April and October and November bring the great waterfowl migrations, but a variety of other birds can be seen in the remaining months. In January and February, especially during a warm spell, one can see diving ducks, rough-legged hawks, short-eared owls, and occasionally, a bald eagle or snowy owl. The beautiful glossy ibis is

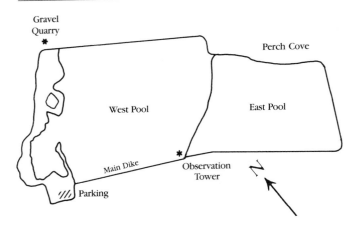

Gravel
Quarry

Perch Cove

West Pool

East Pool

Main Dike

Observation
Tower

Parking

N

abundant in late April, and August heralds the gathering of large numbers of shorebirds and waders.

Follow the auto road past the gate, down around a grassy field, and then turn right onto the main dike. To the left is West Pool, a 900-acre largely freshwater pool. Water control devices along the dike prevent the entrance of salt water from the bay, while allowing fresh water to flow out. The water level in this pool is regulated by refuge managers in order to control plant growth, and to make aquatic foods available to various types of waterfowl.

To the right of you as you walk is an extensive area of salt marsh. Here silt and nutrients from upland runoff were deposited, then stabilized by plants that can tolerate periodic inundation by salt water. The carpetlike plant growing above the high tide line is salt-meadow grass (also called salt-marsh hay). Its weak stems tend to fall over in swirling mats, giving the appearance of grassy cowlicks. In fact, this marsh may have had cows on it at one time, since many farmers along the coast pastured their cows on the salt-meadow grass. Today the plant provides food for geese, muskrat, and meadow voles, who eat the roots as well as the stems.

The other principal plant of the salt marsh is the salt-marsh cordgrass (or thatch grass), which is taller and has stiff round stems and long, coarse, sharply pointed leaves. It can stand more wetness than the salt-meadow grass, and so is usually found growing closer to the water. It provides nesting cover for sharp-tailed and seaside sparrows, both of which also feed on its seeds.

After walking about a mile, you reach a large observation tower, which is definitely worth the climb. On late autumn afternoons, you can watch thousands of brant, Canada geese, and snow geese lift off from bays to the northeast and fly straight toward you before veering off to settle down for a drink in the pool below. The sound of so many birds on such an afternoon is awesome. From the tower also can be seen the changing colors of the marsh. The salt-marsh grasses and reeds are blue green and yellow green in the summer, tawny and gold in the fall, and dun colored in winter. In the middle of summer, the flowers of the salt-marsh hay form violet patches on the marsh.

Continue past the cross dike that separates West Pool from this area of brackish water and low islands, which is managed as a nesting area for a variety of ducks. These islands serve as nest sites, not only for the abundant mallard and black ducks, but for pintails, blue- and green-winged teal, gadwalls, shovelers, and ruddy ducks as well. These last three species traditionally have bred mainly west of the Mississippi, but are now becoming more common as breeders along the Atlantic coast.

Of all the ducks that nest in or visit the refuge, the little ruddy duck may be the most captivating. In spring, the male has a chestnut body, black crown, and white cheeks, and the colorful breeding attire also includes his bill, which is bright blue. Both the male and female ruddy have distinctive long, stiff tails which are often held straight up in the air. During his courtship display, the male raises and spreads his tail, and at the same time produces bubbles by expelling air trapped under his breast feathers. Although the ruddy duck is not a common breeder here, the pools

Snow geese and "blue geese," Edwin B. Forsythe National
Wildlife Refuge   *Courtesy Edwin B. Forsythe National
Wildlife Refuge Staff*

along this section of the road are the best place to witness
this strange display.

A little more than a mile beyond the observation tower,
the road turns to follow the eastern edge of East Pool.
Another 3/4 mile and the road turns again, this time
running parallel to Perch Cove to the right. Stretching out
to the north and east are 16,000 acres of refuge salt marsh
and bays which provide winter habitat for American brant,
a small goose seldom found far from the ocean. Like the
snow goose, it breeds on the Arctic tundra and winters on
a small strip of the Atlantic coast from New Jersey to North
Carolina.

Less than twenty years ago, the brant was faced with
near extinction because of the almost complete destruc-

tion of its winter forage. The brant had traditionally fed almost exclusively on eelgrass, a ribbonlike marine plant, while in its winter quarters. Around 1930, a blight struck the eelgrass, and within a few years most of it had disappeared from the waters of the northeastern seaboard.

Food-habit studies of the brant after 1932 show that this adaptable goose made a tremendous dietary change in response to the decline of its preferred winter forage. Beginning at that time, a marine algae called sea lettuce made up about three-quarters of the brant's diet, and now, while the eelgrass beds are still recovering, this plant continues to be an extremely important winter food for the brant.

The road passes the cross dike, then swings right before turning to follow the northern edge of the freshwater pool. Bits of cattail marsh flank the left side of the road here, and these harbor a variety of wildlife. Muskrat feed on the cattail rootstocks and tubers, while ducks, red-wing blackbirds, and grackles nest among the tall, flexible leaves. Weasels prowl through them, hunting for meadow voles, and mink search the cattail hummocks for mice, frogs, and snakes.

On the other side of the road there is more salt marsh, broken by tidal creeks and mud flats. At low tide this is a good place to see fiddler crabs, which make their burrows in the banks of these tidal inlets. These crabs are hunted by glossy ibis, which can be seen here in large numbers in spring and summer, probing the mud with their long, downturned bill. The ibis is a strikingly colored bird, with rich chestnut plumage and iridescent green wings. Clapper rails, another wading bird that relishes fiddler crabs, nest along here, but these secretive birds are rarely seen.

Another $^1/_2$ mile further, as the road nears the end of the pool, be on the lookout for peregrine falcons. Since 1976, Cornell University has released twenty young peregrines at Brigantine as part of its program to revive the population of this magnificent bird. The large raised platform that can be seen off to the left is one of the release sites, and it was here in the summer of 1980 that the first pair of captive bred peregrines successfully raised their own chick.

Just before the road swings to the left, there is a bluff on the right created by the excavation of sand and gravel used to construct the dikes over which you have been walking. The trees on the bluff frequently serve as roosts for bald eagles. December is the most likely month to see bald eagles here, but they are occasionally seen during January and February.

The road is now firmly on dry land, but even here the water birds dot the landscape. The grassy fields to the left of the road are a favorite grazing area for Canada geese. Beyond these fields, the road leads into deciduous woods, and $1/2$ mile further, reaches the parking area.

Cape May Region

Red-tailed hawk, Cape May Point

28. Moores Beach

Distance: 2 miles (Easy)
Walking time: 2 hours
Directions: From northern New Jersey, take the NJ Turnpike south to exit 3 (Runnemede). Go south (left) on NJ
168 (Black Horse Pike) one mile to NJ 41. Take NJ 41
south 5 miles to NJ 47, and continue straight for about
15 miles, until you reach US 40. Go west (right) on US 40
one mile to NJ 55. Take NJ 55 south for 21 miles to its end
at NJ 47 in Port Elizabeth. Continue south on NJ 47 9 miles
to Moores Beach Rd., which is the first right after Glade
Rd. From the Jersey shore, take the Garden State Parkway
to exit 13. Go west $1/2$ mile to US 9, then turn south (left).
At Swainton, turn west (right) onto county road 646 and
continue until you reach NJ 47 at Goshen. Turn right and
go about 13 miles to Moores Beach Rd. Go a little less than
a mile along Moores Beach Rd. Just past the last house, the
blacktop ends and there is a wide place in the dirt road
where you may park.

The Delaware Bayshore is "land's end" of a sort, where
forest yields to the open sky of extensive salt marshes,
sandy beaches, and the bay itself. It is a region infrequently
visited, except by duckhunters and birdwatchers, southern
New Jersey sun seekers passing it by for the more familiar
terrain of Wildwood and Cape May. But it is a region with
a distinct flavor that is well worth sampling, and the
Moores Beach walk is only one of many possibilities. As
"land's end," this and any other walks in the area are
necessarily out-and-back excursions; circuit hikes are made
impossible by the countless meandering creeks that divide
the Bayshore. This walk takes place in the Heislerville
Wildlife Management Area, a 4000-acre unit of formerly
diked salt-hay marshes, manmade ponds, tidal marsh, and
pine and oak woods.

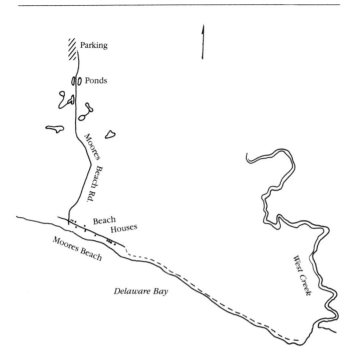

Begin your walk where the asphalt road turns to dirt. During the spring and fall migrations, the ponds on either side of the road here attract a wide variety of shorebirds. Though the majority of these are en route to or from the northern reaches of North America, there are also visitors from across the Atlantic. The ruff, which gets its name from the male's showy breeding plumage, is a regular sight at this pond in the fall. The shorebirds are joined by a number of different ducks, both during migration and in winter, and three terns—Forster's, black, and Caspian—can be seen in flight over this area.

It is a little under a mile to the shore, and along the way, what at first glance appears to be an unvarying landscape of salt hay (salt-meadow cordgrass, with the taller, coarser salt-marsh cordgrass flanking the tidal guts) increasingly comes alive with birdlife. Herons and egrets stalk the shallows along the tidal creeks, harriers hover or sail over the seemingly endless meadows of salt hay, and occasionally one foraging harrier runs across another's path, and their long even soar is punctuated with a flurry of "out of my way" erratic flight. Overhead pass a constant volley of snow geese, and if you look to the eastern or western horizon, the rising flocks of geese and ducks often are so thick that they resemble swarms of insects. (*Real* swarms of biting insects replace the geese in summer; come prepared!)

Though the variety and number of waterfowl is less in winter months than the rest of the season, it is an ideal time for this walk. A sunny January day, even when temperatures are in the thirties and there is a stiff breeze out of the west, warms most walkers. Once you reach the beach, it is possible to find a sheltering dune and duck the wind a little. A winter walk allows you to avoid the fall hunting season as well.

When you reach the beach, turn left and follow the road past a group of cabins and trailers to its end. Swing out onto the beach and continue walking until you reach the mouth of a tidal creek. In May, the mud flats here at low tide harbor the largest concentrations of migrant shorebirds along the east coast of North America. Along with the tens of thousands of ruddy turnstones, red knots, sanderlings, semipalmated sandpipers, and other "peeps," the area hosts such rarities as white ibis, black-necked stilt, curlew sandpiper, and northern wheatear. Flocks of brown pelicans have been spotted offshore.

At any season, by now you will have passed plenty of evidence of one of the key reasons that the Delaware Bayshore is so attractive to these migrant shorebirds—horseshoe crabs. Every May countless numbers of these armor-plated creatures make their way to this and other Bayshore beaches to lay their eggs, which at low tide are left exposed to the hungry migrants. The horseshoe crabs shed a series of shells as they grow, and many of the spent shells you will see on your walk are empty juvenile shells, not the remains of dead adults. Another shell occasionally turns up on this walk—the shell of the diamondback terrapin.

A close examination of these two magnificently designed protective devices will reveal some striking comparisons and contrasts. The horseshoe crab shell is much thinner and lighter than that of the terrapin, and if you crack open part of the horseshoe's armor you'll see that it is porous. The irregular reinforcement between the upper and lower shells is reminiscent of the structure of bird bones—both are rigid, but lightweight. The terrapin's shell, on the other hand, is a densely packed mass of cells, whose growth is marked by tight concentric rings. (These rings can actually be felt as slight ridges on the shell surface.) Notice how the scutes (plates) of the terrapin's shell join in such a way as always to form 120° angles; the same pattern can be seen in miniature on the surface of the horseshoe crab shell. The tiny sets of lines etched on the horseshoe shell are telltales of wrinkles that once covered the shell while it was still new, yet to be born from under the old, ready-to-moult shell. After this old shell is shed, the new shell expands and then stiffens, and only these scars remain to speak of its wrinkled state.

Once your eyes have accustomed themselves to seeing these 120° junctions, you will no doubt begin to see them elsewhere on your walk. As the mudflats bake in the sun and dry out at low tide, the cracks in the mud form these three-way junctions. The froth left on the beach by incoming waves takes the same shape. If you should come upon any surfaces packed with barnacles, they too will form triple junctions. Even the Atlantic coastline shows traces of this ubiquitous geometry. Long Island Sound and the Connecticut River occupy two arms of an ancient triple junction produced by the separation of the earth's crust at the margins of the North American tectonic plate.

They all result from one of nature's fundamental design problems—how to minimize work or energy in the production of surfaces. Whether produced by cracking, packing, wrinkling, or surface tension, three lines are the fewest that can be brought together at any point to subdivide a plane surface. Hence the triple junction.

On your return walk, consider the fact that humans are not removed from nature's economy. The human brain, like the terrapin's and horseshoe crab's shell, produces wrinkles as it grows, and thus shares a surface symmetry with some of the objects it contemplates.

29. Cape May City

Distance: 2¹/₂ miles (Easy)
Walking time: 3 hours
Directions: Take the Garden State Parkway south to the
end, then continue on Lafayette St. toward Cape May City.
Turn left on Union St., then right onto Washington St. Park
at the Emlen Physick Estate (Cape May Museum), 1048
Washington St.

Considering the development of the New Jersey coast
from Asbury Park to Atlantic City, it is remarkable that the
historic seashore resort of Cape May survives. Though it
has changed a great deal in the past 100 years, Cape May
retains much of its nineteenth-century charm: its beautiful
Victorian buildings, many of which are still used for their
original purposes; its size, being still a walkable city; and
its slower, less commercial pace. A walking tour is the
most enjoyable way to see Cape May, and the one presented here is meant as a beginning for more extensive
rambles around this, the nation's oldest seashore resort.

The walk begins at the Emlen Physick house, which is
open daily in the summer and varied hours from mid-
October to mid-March. (Call 609-884-5404 for hours during
the off season, which is recommended for this walk, since
crowds of visitors are easily avoided.) The peculiarities of
the house's design—oversized dormers and chimneys that
broaden as they extend above the roof—are popularly
attributed to the eccentricity of its owner, Emlen Physick.
However, these features were not uncommon in nineteenth-century architecture. The architect, Frank Furness,
built a number of houses of similar design in Philadelphia
at around the same time that he designed the Physick
house (1870).

From the Physick house, walk four blocks along Wash-

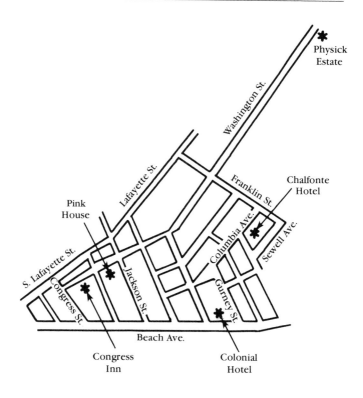

Physick
Estate

Washington St.

Chalfonte
Hotel

Franklin St.

Lafayette St.

Pink
House

Columbia Ave.

Sewell Ave.

S. Lafayette St.

Jackson St.

Congress St.

Gurney St.

Beach Ave.

Congress
Inn

Colonial
Hotel

ington Street to Franklin Street and turn right. On the left along the last block (720 Washington Street) is the George Allen house, now called Victorian House. Built for Allen, a Philadelphia merchant, in 1863-1864, the house is one of the most elaborate that survives in Cape May. Five-foot-high brackets support a gigantic roof, which in turn supports a large, richly ornamented cupola. The opulence outside is reflected within the house, where marble fireplaces and foot-wide moldings delight the eye.

From Franklin Street, turn left onto Lafayette Street. The bandstand on your left at Decatur Street is not an authentic Victorian structure, but was built in 1974. Patterned after a bandstand in Sefton Park in Liverpool, England, it was designed with the structural elements of Victorian wood-work instead of the cast-iron members that adorned the original. Almost directly across the street from the band-stand is the Cape May Island Presbyterian Church, whose Georgian-vernacular facade contrasts with the unusual onion-domed, vaguely oriental cupola that towers above the building. Erected in 1853, the building served the congregation until 1898, when a new church was built; today, the Cape May Community Center is located here.

Just past the community center, turn left onto Jackson Street, and then right into the pedestrian mall that is an extension of Washington Street. Ahead lies the impressive Congress Hall and the row of lovely homes along Congress Place. At the end of the mall, cross Perry Street onto Congress Place and then look back to your left and notice the pink building. This is the Eldridge Johnson house, now called the Pink House, which was built around 1880. The Pink House is probably the most elaborately decorated cottage in Cape May, its gingerbread woodwork looking like a huge veil draped in front of the building.

On the left looms Congress Hall, a large L-shaped hotel facing the ocean. This building is actually the third on this site to have that name; the first, built around 1812, was one of the earliest hotels in Cape May. Rebuilt and mod-ernized in the 1850s, Congress Hall was destroyed in the 1878 fire that burned thirty acres of the city, and then was rebuilt again in 1879.

Across the street are three homes built about the same time as the new Congress Hall—in fact, these homes are located on the site of the old hotel, which after the fire was relocated closer to the ocean. The middle building, the Joseph Evans house (identified by a black cast-iron widow's walk flanked by two chimneys), was designed by Stephen Decatur Button, Cape May's most prolific and noted architect. Between 1863 and 1893, Button designed more than forty of the resort's buildings. His impact on the architecture of the town goes beyond the buildings he

E. C. Knight house, Cape May City

designed, however, since many of the local builders copied his work quite closely.

At the end of the block lies the E. C. Knight house, which may also have been designed by Button. Knight was one of the many influential Philadelphians who summered in Cape May—these merchants and bankers, lured by booming land values as much as by the sand and sea, directed much of the town's economic and physical growth. To a considerable extent this growth, like that in any resort town, has been dependent on the type of transportation available to potential visitors. Located at the confluence of the Atlantic Ocean and the Delaware River, Cape May was in the early 1800s only a river cruise from Philadelphia, and a relatively short distance (across Delaware Bay) from such urban centers as Washington, D.C. and Baltimore. In the middle of the 1800s steamboats and then trains kept Cape May within reach, although the railroad had reached Atlantic City before Cape May, and that resort's growth began to eclipse Cape May's around 1862.

Before turning onto Congress Street, note the twin cottages straight ahead. Built around 1850 for two brothers, Joseph and John Steiner, these two buildings were among the first summer cottages built in Cape May. Up until 1850, tourists usually depended on hotels and rooming houses for their lodging, but the increase in personal wealth that began in the late 1800s led to a trend toward privately owned summer homes.

Turning left onto South Lafayette Street, you pass the Joseph Leedham house, located at the corner of South Lafayette and Congress streets. Round fish-scale-shingled towers, boldly projecting bays, and a complex asymmetry distinguish the house as being of the style known as Queen Anne. In many Cape May buildings of the 1870s and 1880s the Queen Anne influence appeared mainly in the form of towers added to conventional summer cottages, but the Leedham house, designed by Philadelphia architect Charles Collum in 1883, integrates many Queen Anne fashions into the overall building.

Turn left onto Windsor Avenue and follow it out to Beach Avenue. As you turn left onto Beach, you will notice the beachfront facade of Congress Hall. The L-shaped plan of the hotel gives the maximum number of rooms an ocean view. The construction of Beach Avenue and a boardwalk in 1869 were important developments in Cape May's history, as they assured access to the ocean for the general public. Before the road and nearby buildings could be constructed, however, sand dunes had to be leveled and large areas of wetland filled in. These dunes and marshes once served as buffers against the fierce storms that ravaged this area periodically, and with their destruction, the waves whipped up by northeasters were free to batter the growing resort town. Most recently, a storm in

Cape May City 219

October 1980 caused hundreds of thousands of dollars worth of damage to property along the beachfront.

At the corner of Beach Avenue and Ocean Street, you pass the Colonial Hotel. Built in 1894, the Colonial was considered extremely modern in its time, featuring steam heat, gaslights, electric bells for room service, and the very first elevator in Cape May. Like Congress Hall, it also advertised "superb ocean views from nearly every room."

Turn left onto Gurney Street; the houses along the left side of the street were designed by Button in 1869 and were collectively christened Stockton Place, in honor of the Stockton Hotel which was then located across the street. Although they are fairly typical Cape May cottages, some of the buildings are distinguished by their elaborate wood ornamentation. The Baldt house, located at 26 Gurney Street, retains all of its original woodwork, including the large wooden acroterion atop the roof peak. Others of the cottages have been modified a great deal: gingerbread has been removed, porches have been simplified, and shingles have been changed. The cottage next to the Baldt house has been almost totally rebuilt into a 1920s shingle-style house; its tall, narrow proportions and gable angles, however, identify it unmistakably as one of the original Stockton Place cottages.

At the end of Stockton Place is the fantastic John B. McCreary house (now The Abbey, a guest house). In 1869 McCreary, a wealthy coal baron and politician, commissioned Button to design a summer villa for him in Cape May. The result was a building so unusual that the *Cape May Ocean Wave* was prompted to comment on its style: "Elizabethan, Gothic, and Doric and a description of it so as to convey an idea of what it looks like would occupy more space than we have at our disposal this week." An imposing tower, stenciled and ruby glass windows, and the repetition of the Gothic arch in the doors, windows, and porch brackets are among the features that distinguish the McCreary house.

Turn right on Columbia Avenue, passing the Victorian mansion (now the Mainstay Inn) on the left. Originally known as Jackson's Clubhouse, the building is another Button design, built in 1872 for Col. Charles Jackson, a wealthy gambler from New York. Its stately porch, large veranda, and pilastered cupola distinguish it outside. Inside, the house is even more handsome, graced by fourteen-foot ceilings, ornate plaster moldings, and elaborate chandeliers. Many of the original furnishings remain in the house, and these can be seen on the guided tours which are offered from May through November.

Turn left onto Stockton Place and then right on Hughes Street, passing a number of houses built between 1868 and 1872. The Joseph Hall house (645 Hughes) has distinctive vinelike woodwork on the main dormer, but is otherwise somewhat plain. The J. Stratton Ware house (653–655 Hughes) is much more elaborate, with ornate barge boards, incised carvings, and acroteria crowning the dormers.

To return to the Physick house and your car, turn left on Franklin Street, then right onto Washington Street.

30. Cape May Point State Park

Distance: 2 miles (Easy)
Walking time: 1 hour
Directions: Take the Garden State Parkway south to the end, then continue on Lafayette St. to Cape May City. Turn right on Perry, which then becomes West Sunset Blvd., and after going 2 miles turn left on Lighthouse Ave. The park entrance is $^3/_4$ mile down on the left. The half-mile boardwalk portion of this walk is designed specifically for wheelchair access. (609) 884-2159

For many people, Cape May is synonymous with birds. Since records were first maintained, over 400 species of birds have been recorded at Cape May, making it one of the most famous places to observe birds in all of North America. Particularly spectacular at Cape May is the autumn hawk migration: from early September to late November, hundreds of hawks can be seen each day and on good days, hawks number in the thousands. In 1977, a total of 81,597 hawks were seen from the observation area at Cape May Point State Park, a national record for the most hawks recorded from a single point during an autumn migration.

Cape May is a long, narrow extension of the Outer Coastal Plain, and is bordered by Delaware Bay on the west and the Atlantic Ocean on the east. Because many birds are hesitant to cross large stretches of open water, Cape May's geography makes it a natural funnel, catching southbound landbirds and channeling them to its terminus at Cape May Point. A walk through Cape May Point State Park then, no matter what the season, is highlighted by the abundant and varied birdlife, but you need not be a birdwatcher to enjoy this unique area.

From the parking lot, walk to the trail entrance at the

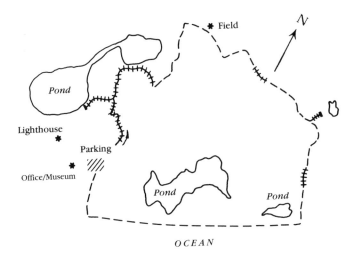

left rear corner of the lot. The trail is flanked by phragmites, groundsel-tree, elderberry, wax myrtle, and bayberry. These last two shrubs are closely related and are similar in appearance: both have egg-shaped, slightly toothed leaves that have minute resin dots on the surface. These resin dots account for the strong scent of the leaves when they are crushed. Wax myrtle's leathery leaves stay on the plant all year long, while the bayberry is deciduous; it is also distinguished by being less shrubby in its growth habit.

The most conspicuous similarity in the two plants is their small, wax-covered nutlets, or berries, which hug the twigs. These berries were commonly harvested during colonial days to make scented candles, as some enterprising people still do today. (A pound of nutlets immersed in hot water yields four ounces of wax.) Today, most of the harvesting is done by myrtle warblers (now officially known as yellow-rumped warblers) who during their fall migration light by the thousands to feed on the bayberries. The myrtle warbler can be seen here through January and

February, as it is the only warbler that regularly spends the winter this far north.

The principal tree in the open sections of the park is the eastern red cedar, which is recognized by its dry, papery bark that shreds to reveal the reddish heartwood below. Its dark green needles are of two different kinds: some are sharply pointed, while others, particularly on older trees, are flattened and overlapping. The fruit is a hard, bluish berry that is covered with a whitish bloom. The red cedar is the most widely distributed conifer of tree size in the eastern United States, growing under a wide variety of soil and climatic conditions. The tenacity that makes it such an aggressive colonizer of abandoned fields further north serves it as well on the dry, windswept coastal sands here.

The trail then forks. Bear left here onto the red-blazed trail. The boardwalk soon emerges from a growth of cedars and comes upon an area that was once a pond, then filled in with vegetation to become an open meadow, and has since been taken over by tall phragmites. This is a good spot to glance up, as sharp-shinned and marsh hawks stream by overhead. The number of hawks depends to a large degree on the weather conditions. Generally, good hawk flights follow the passage of a cold front, when a low-pressure system moves off the New England coast, while a high-pressure system moves out of Canada. Such a weather system produces northwest winds, which blow inland migrants toward the coast, concentrating them in the numbers that make hawk watching at Cape May so spectacular.

Along the following section of boardwalk there is a small detour to the left which leads to a platform overlooking a freshwater pond. Painted turtles sun themselves here while mallards and black ducks float lazily along the surface. If you look very carefully you may see a least bittern as it skulks through the cattails and reed grass that ring the outer edge of the pond. This small, extremely

Cape May lighthouse with ruins, since washed away, of old lighthouse in foreground, Cape May State Park

secretive heron has a blackish back and conspicuous buff wing patches and underparts.

The trail passes into a wooded area, where it joins the blue and yellow trail; turn left here (Wheelchairs must turn right and follow the boardwalk back to the beginning.). After passing back into the open, the trail enters a wooded section again, where sweet gum and sassafras are the principal trees. Sassafras is easily identified by its sweet-smelling leaves, which occur in three different shapes. Most commonly the leaves are oval, but they are less commonly divided into three lobes; occasionally they are two lobed or mitten shaped. On older trees the bark is a deeply furrowed orange brown, and the new shoots are bright yellowish green. In fall, the leaves of the sassafras turn brilliant colors, ranging from yellow through orange and even pink.

After about $1/4$ mile the trail passes an open field, which can be seen through the bushes on the left. In the fall, the Cape May Bird Observatory, the research arm of the New Jersey Audubon Society, uses this field as part of its banding operation. If you remain hidden along the edge of the woods, you'll see what appears to be an injured pigeon flapping about on the ground. The pigeon is actually tethered to serve as a lure for hawks flying overhead, who swoop down to capture the "injured" bird, only to be caught in the observatory's nets. These hawks are then marked with a small aluminum leg band, which will serve to provide information for bird migration and population studies should the hawk be recaptured at a future date.

The trail passes back into the woods, which on days with very strong northwest winds, may be filled with half a dozen hawks perched quietly in the black cherry trees. On such extremely windy days, many hawks are reluctant to fly, and take cover in wooded sections like this one. The trail shortly leaves the woods and crosses a marshy area covered by phragmites before returning through a wooded section.

About $1/8$ mile into the woods, there is a short detour to the left to an observation platform overlooking a small pond. The pond is again ringed by phragmites, but just beyond is a small cattail marsh. In spring, this marsh is alive with the sights and sounds of redwing blackbirds, who build their cup-shaped nests amid the tall cattail leaves. The territorial males can be seen flying above the marsh calling loudly while displaying their brilliant red shoulder patches or epaulets. These red epaulets contrast sharply with the all-black plumage of the rest of the redwing's body, and like many such color patches, they serve as a means of communication. When the male redwing flashes his brightly colored epaulets, they are as effective as his throaty call in advertising his presence to competing males.

Directly in front of the platform can be seen the cone-shaped house of a muskrat. The muskrat house is built of piled-up cattail stalks, roots, plant remains, and mud which is dug from the area around the house foundation. The mainly nocturnal muskrat is active throughout the year and is sometimes seen during the daytime building houses, swimming, or sunning itself. The stems, leaves, and roots of many marsh plants, particularly cattail, form the bulk of the muskrat's diet.

Just before the trail leaves the woods, it reaches an intersection with a yellow-blazed trail; go straight. The trail follows through more phragmites before reaching a brackish pond. Here salt water has invaded, and instead of being surrounded by cattail and reed grass, the marshy area around the pond consists of spike grass and salt-meadow grass.

After crossing the dune, turn right and follow the beach. This is a good area to look for Cape May diamonds, actually quartz pebbles that have been polished smooth by thousands of years of weathering and abrasion. The "diamonds" vary from the size of tiny peas to, quite rarely, the size of a chicken's egg, and are usually colorless, though some are tinted yellow or amber. Cape May diamonds are thought to be derived from the sands and gravels deposited throughout southern New Jersey during the Pleistocene. These sands and gravels are largely stained yellow from limonite, but some of the pebbles from deposits that have been washed into the sea have had this limonite coating removed by natural abrasion. (Limonite-stained sands can be seen along exposed sections of this beach.)

As you walk along the dunes, keep an eye out for migrating falcons: kestrels, merlins, and peregrines. Unlike the buteos and accipiter hawks, these strong fliers with scimitar-shaped wings prefer to migrate along the coast. The sight of a feisty merlin or peregrine winging low over the dunes in pursuit of a migrating shorebird is a sight not soon forgotten.

Cape May Point State Park 227

The large concrete structure being undermined by the sea is the remains of a United States army artillery unit built during World War II. The ocean has had severe effects on the dunes near here as well. Just beyond the bunker lies an area of sand dune which was blown out during a northeast storm in the fall of 1980. The freshwater pond formerly protected from the sea was invaded by salt water, making the pond brackish in some sections.

Continue down the beach. Until the winter of 1982–1983 you could see the remains of an earlier lighthouse a short distance ahead. This lighthouse (the ruins appear in the photograph on page 219) was built in 1847, after the sea had encroached on the first lighthouse, built over $1/3$ of a mile to the south in 1823. In 1982 the same erosional forces that have twice required the relocation of the Cape May lighthouse removed the evidence of the 1847 structure.

Continue along the beach until you see the trail that returns to the parking lot. If it's a good day, you might like to stop at the observation platform located near the parking area. From the first of September through the last of November, observers from the Cape May Bird Observatory are here counting hawks, and an hour or so spent with them can be an excellent introduction to hawk identification.

Geologic Timetable

Glossary

Geologic Timetable

Era	Period	Epoch	Millions of years ago
Cenezoic	Quaternary	Recent	
		Pleistocene (The Great Ice Age)	2.5
	Tertiary	Pliocene	7
		Miocene	26
		Oligocene	38
		Eocene	54
		Paleocene	65
Mesozoic	Cretaceous		
			136
	Jurassic		
			190
	Triassic		
			225
Paleozoic	Permian		280
	Pennsylvanian		320
	Mississippian		345
	Devonian		395
	Silurian		440

Global geological/biological events	New Jersey rocks
Many large Ice Age mammals become extinct.	Present-day stream deposits, beaches.
Continental glaciation; origin of human beings.	Glacial deposits in north; yellow gravels in central and south.
Mammals at height. Rocky Mts. born (75 million years ago).	Unconsolidated sediments of the N.J. coastal plain.
Extinction of dinosaurs; origin of flowering plants.	Unconsolidated sediments of northwestern part of the N.J. coastal plain.
Breakup of Pangaea—N.A., Africa, and Eurasia drift apart; origin of birds.	Palisades disturbance.
Rise of dinosaurs; origin of mammals	Red shales, sandstones, argillites, basalt extrusives, and diabase intrusives of the Newark basin.
Origin of reptiles.	Not present in N.J.
Great fern forests; coal deposits of Pennsylvania	Not present in N.J.
	Not present in N.J.
Origin of amphibians; age of fishes.	Upper Delaware limestone, Bearfort Mt. conglomerate.
First land plants	High Falls sandstone in Northwest N.J., conglomerate in Green Pond Valley (Morris and Passaic counties).

Geologic Timetable 231

Era	Period	Epoch	Millions of years ago
	Ordovician		500
	Cambrian		570

Precambrian

Global geological/biological events	*New Jersey rocks*
Extensive warm, shallow seas; trilobites.	Shales and limestones of Kittatinny Ridge. Limestone and sandstone in Sussex and Warren counties.
Oldest fossils (3.5 billion years old). Oldest rocks (4.1 billion years old).	Gneiss and other metamorphic rocks, Franklin marble in N.J. Highlands.

Glossary

accipiter: any of a group of hawks characterized by long tails, short, rounded wings, and low darting flight

alluvial: soil deposited by running water

alternate (leaves, buds): not opposite, but arranged singly at intervals along twigs

argillite: a compact, clay-containing rock having no slaty cleavage

barrier beach: a low island of sand built by waves, parallel to the shore, and separated from it by a lagoon or shallow bay

basalt: a dark gray to black fine-grained igneous rock

bedrock: the solid rock underlying unconsolidated surface materials (i.e. soil)

bog: a poorly drained, acidic wetland, rich in organic remains (plant residues)

boreal: northern

bottomland: low-lying, moist area along streams and rivers

bract: a modified leaf that encloses another structure, usually a flower

buteo: any of a group of hawks characterized by broad wings and tail, and soaring flight

canopy: the uppermost layer of foliage in a forest

carapace: the horny or bony protective covering over the back of an animal (e.g. a turtle's shell)

catkin: cluster of tiny flowers or fruits, usually fuzzy and caterpillar shaped (such as those of willows)

climax: the final stage in the succession of plants in a particular setting of soil and climate

compound (leaf): one composed of separate leaflets, each of which usually looks like a single leaf (ash, hickory)

conglomerate: a sedimentary rock composed of rounded fragments varying from small pebbles to large boulders within a matrix of sandstone

conifer: a member of an order (Coniferales) of trees and shrubs having evergreen foliage and bearing seeds in a cone (pine, cedar, etc.)

deciduous: a tree that is not an evergreen, but loses its leaves seasonally, usually in autumn

diabase: a finely crystalline igneous rock

dominant: any plant that predominates in a community by height, size, and number

dorsal: related to the back of an animal

drift: unsorted rock debris deposited by a glacier

endemic: limited in distribution to a particular region or habitat

epoch: a division of geologic time less than a period

estuary: the lower end of a river that meets the sea

extrusive: formed by crystallization of lava poured out at the earth's surface

fault: a fracture in the earth's crust accompanied by lateral displacements of the opposing sides of the fracture

floodplain: level land that is seasonally inundated by floodwaters

floret: a single small flower within a group of similar small flowers

flyway: an established air route of migratory birds

fold: a bend produced in rock by geologic forces

formation: any consecutive series of rock layers homogeneous enough to be a unit

fungus: any of a large group of plants, including mushrooms, molds, and the like, that lack chlorophyll and reproduce by means of spores

genus: a group of species sufficiently closely related to be given the same (Latin) generic name

glacier: a large body of ice spreading outward on a land surface

gneiss: a coarse-grained metamorphic rock with a banded appearance

granite: a very hard igneous rock consisting mainly of quartz

habitat: the place in which a plant or animal naturally lives and grows

heath: any of a family of plants that thrive on open, barren, often acidic soil

herbaceous: plants having little or no woody tissue and persisting usually for a single growing season

hyphae: the individual tubelike threads of a fungus

igneous: pertaining to rock formed by the process of hot magma cooling above or below the earth's surface *insectivorous*: depending on insects for food

intermittent stream: one that dries up seasonally

lenticel: a circular or stripelike corky spot on the bark originating as a breathing pore

lichen: a plant made up of an alga and fungus growing in symbiotic association

limestone: rock formed chiefly by accumulation of organic remains (e.g. shells, coral)

limonite: a compound of iron oxide and water

lithify: to become rock

lobed (leaf): divided into rounded incompletely separated sections

magma: molten rock material within the earth

magnetite: a black iron oxide mineral

mantle: unconsolidated material overlying bedrock

metamorphic: rock that has been deformed by intense heat and pressure within the earth's crust

microclimate: the uniform local climate of a small site or habitat

midden: a refuse heap

moraine: an accumulation of earth and stones carried and finally deposited by a glacier

nymph: a larva of an insect

opposite (leaves, buds): in opposing pairs

outcrop: an exposure of bare rock; a place where underlying rock protrudes from the soil

peat: an accumulation of partially decomposed organic material

peneplain: a large expanse of gently rolling land

period: a division of geologic time longer than an epoch and included in an era

pH: the measure of acidity or alkalinity

pinnae: leaflets of a pinnate leaf or frond

pinnate: having the leaflets placed at opposite points on the stem

primaries: the principal flight feathers of a bird's wing

quartz: a transparent or colored mineral (SiO_2) occurring in hexagonal crystals or crystalline masses

quartzite: a compact granular rock composed of quartz and derived from sandstone by metamorphism

raptor: a bird of prey

relict: a persistent remnant of an otherwise extinct flora or fauna

riparian: of or relating to or living on the bank of a river

rosette: a cluster of leaves in crowded circles or spirals

samara: a dry, usually one-seeded winged fruit (e.g. those of ash or maple)

sandstone: a sedimentary rock usually made up of quartz sand

scree: rock fragments at the base of a cliff

scute: a small horny or bony plate

sedimentary rock: rock formed of mechanical, chemical, or organic sediment

shale: an easily fragmented rock formed by the consolidation of clay, mud, or silt

sill: a body of igneous rock injected while molten into some other type of rock

sinus: a deep indentation in the margin of a leaf

slate: a dense, fine-grained metamorphic rock usually produced by compression of shale

snag: the standing remains of a dead or dying tree

spadix: a fleshy spike in which florets are embedded

spathe: a large bract around a flower

spore: the reproductive body (asexual) of a primitive plant or fungus

stamen: the male or pollen-bearing part of a flower

striation: scratch made in rock by glacial movement of rock material

succession: the natural process by which plant communities replace one another

talons: claws

talus: rock fragments at the base of a cliff

taproot: a primary root that grows straight down

tendril: a clasping, twining slender outgrowth of the stem

till: unstratified, unsorted rocks, gravel, and debris deposited by a glacier

traprock: various dark-colored, fine-grained igneous rocks (such as basalt or diabase)

understory: the layer of forest growth below the canopy

Index

knot, red, 212

larch, American, 43; European, 161
laurel, mountain, 17, 31, 45, 49, 50, 162; sheep, 13, 168, 174
Lenape, 3, 34, 46, 55, 136–137, 194–195
Lewis, Clarence M., 40
lichens, 12
lilies: wild calla, 38; yellow pond, 37
linden. *See* basswood
lizard, northern fence, 163
locust, black, 73, 83
loosestrife, purple-flowered, 51

magnetite. *See* iron ore
magnolia: sweet bay, 44, 174; umbrella, 161, 162 (photo)
maple: ash-leaf, 104, 105, 106; red, 37, 90, 100, 122, 143, 161; silver, 104, 106, 113; striped, 13–14, 37; sugar, 24, 27, 30, 37, 42, 60, 68
marl, 130
mayapple, 97, 99 (photo), 105
mayflower, Canada, 20, 44, 148
meadowlark, 89
mica, 87
microclimate, 19
moonseed, Canada, 106
Mount Holly, 161
mulberry, 77
muskrat, 89, 227
Musconetcong River, 58

nettle, 112
New England Upland physiographic province, 3
nighthawk, 91

nuthatch, 23

oak: black, 14, 60, 96, 98, 162, 166, 174; blackjack, 166; chestnut, 14–15, 17, 27, 29, 49, 63, 144; dwarf chinquapin, 167; pin, 92, 98, 104–105; post, 166; red, 14, 60, 84, 96, 98, 122, 148; scarlet, 84; scrub, 13, 17, 30, 51, 167; white, 17, 60, 84, 90, 96, 98, 124, 127, 144, 148
opossum, 85
orache, 147
orchid: pink lady's slippers, 21; rattlesnake plantain, 44
osprey, 117, 146
owl: short-eared, 202; snowy, 202

Palisades, 3
partridgeberry, 20, 44, 70
peat, 16
pelican, brown, 212
persimmon, 163
pine: pitch, 13, 17, 29, 51, 144, 166, 168, 174; red, 19, 43, 122; Virginia, 163; white, 19, 43, 107
physiographic provinces of New Jersey, 2–4
pickerelweed, 37, 67 (photo)
Piedmont physiographic province, 3
Pine Barrens, 4, 166
porcupine, 29
prickly pear, 181
pitcher plant, 16
pothole, 23

Quakers, 127, 150
Queen Anne's lace, 160

raccoon, 85